Octave Thanet

A Slave to Duty and Other Women

Octave Thanet

A Slave to Duty and Other Women

ISBN/EAN: 9783744708876

Printed in Europe, USA, Canada, Australia, Japan

Cover: Foto ©ninafisch / pixelio.de

More available books at **www.hansebooks.com**

A SLAVE TO DUTY
& OTHER WOMEN

A
SLAVE TO DUTY

&

OTHER WOMEN

BY

OCTAVE THANET

HERBERT S. STONE & COMPANY
CHICAGO & NEW YORK
MDCCCXCVIII

CONTENTS

	PAGE
A Slave to Duty	1
A Colonial Dame	55
A Jealous Woman	87
A Problem in Honor	131
On the Blank Side of the Wall	185

A Slave to Duty

FRANK MALLORY was fond of his mother-in-law. He was as delighted as a boy when he could get away from the pressure of a great business and spend a few days in the little New England village where Mrs. Wilder had lived ever since the captain's death. In fact, Mrs. Wilder was born in Jeffries. She was born a Jeffries, one of the good old family from which the town was named; and she had never left the town for any long interval, except during the five years of her married life. She married a naval officer, who made her very happy and left her with two little girls and his pension.

She went back to Jeffries, and somehow managed to buy a house out of the pension, and by taking a few boarders among the boys attending the famous Jeffries Academy.

That was how Frank had met and loved

Nora, his wife. That was how the other son-in-law—but they never talked of the other son-in-law.

After Frank's wonderful prosperity in business Nora had prevailed on her mother at odd times to accept certain stocks and bonds and other personal estate, which had been so wisely invested that Mrs. Wilder was very comfortable, and quite able, as she told Frank, often—oh, quite able to care for Wait! She would not build a new house. She enlarged and beautified the old walls, but she would not have new.

To-day, as Frank leaned back in the old leather chair, he could see some of the same furniture that he had known in the days when he had courted Nora; and Wait had comforted his boyish jealousies. Its presence did not embarrass the new furniture, for it was old and of no pretense, and rather gave notice that its owners had been gentle-folks in another century. Nora herself, handsomer in her dark, vivacious beauty than when she was his sweetheart, sat on the piano-stool, throwing her words and her flashing smile over her shoulder at her mother and Frank. Mrs. Wilder was the image of a placid, sweet-natured gentlewoman, softly shimmering in grays, with crisp white tulle at her throat and in her widow's cap. Wait was standing at the piano. She had her mother's dove's eyes and delicately fair skin, and her mother's slim grace and sweet expression; but she had never been pretty, like her mother—only what the Jeffries people called "nice looking." She had been singing the Easter hymns over with Nora, Mrs. Wilder joining them occasionally in a thin, sweet, true treble, and Frank listening. He extended his immaculate lavender trousers, and peacefully surveyed his varnished shoes. His large frame had relaxed every muscle. His keen gray eyes were beaming with lazy kindness, and he smiled under his brown mustache so benevolently that one would hardly notice the bold outline of his shaven jaws and his Roman nose. Nobody, he least of all, would have pictured this genial image breaking the ten commandments and the laws of his country before sunset. That is because we are not prophets.

A SLAVE TO DUTY

Close to Frank, rubbing his cheek against the big man's knee, sat a boy of six, whose unhappy fate was written on his face, in the low forehead, vacant eyes and sagging mouth; yet he was not otherwise repulsive Indeed, he wore a smile of timid good-will that excited good-will and compassion in return. While the others were busied at the piano, he plucked at Frank's sleeve and showed him something hidden under the chair. He chuckled and cooed like a baby of two, then, instantly, made a face of exaggerated warning.

"What are you after, old man?" said Frank, lazily.

Wait instantly turned her head. Any one who saw her could tell that she was his mother, and that her soul was bound up in him.

"Maybe he wants his own hymn," she said; "he can tell the difference, and always knows his own." She began to sing:

> "Onward, Christian soldier,
> Marching as for war."

But the boy, although apparently listening to the hymn, slyly nipped his uncle's leg and

A SLAVE TO DUTY

displayed his treasure. His mother detected the action.

"What is he trying to show you? Why, Bertie, you aren't playing boat on Sunday?"

Bertie hung his head, but his mother crossed the room to kiss him, and her face was alight.

"See, mother," she cried, joyously, "he knows the difference; he knows he is doing wrong!" And she kissed him again.

"It does show reason," said Mrs. Wilder, a little dubiously.

"Of course it does," Frank agreed, in a confident tone. "He actually pinched my leg to get me onto his little game."

"You are so good to him, Frank," said Wait; "but truly, don't you think he understands? and he knows a good many more words all the time."

"Oh, he's coming on," said Frank, "and the boat is a nice boat for *any* boy of six to make. It's neatly done, remarkably neatly done."

"He does everything so neatly," said his mother. "Why, he can sew a seam on the machine so you can use it, and he doesn't mind doing anything over and over again until he has it right. Come, Bertie, let us go out to walk."

"Uncle Nice," said Bertie, slowly, pulling at Frank's sleeve.

"No, dearie, Uncle Nice must stay and talk to grandma."

Bertie submitted with his usual docility; but before he went he threw his arms around his uncle's neck and kissed him. Wait was looking; her pale face flushed up to her eyebrows, as she involuntarily extended her hand to draw Bertie away. But Frank kissed the little fellow on his cheek, and patted his shoulder and frankly wiped his own cheek, smiling and saying:

"That was what I call a large, round, loud kiss. Here, give me a small, square, soft kiss—like this."

Wait watched Bertie obey and laugh delightedly at his uncle's approval. "I don't wonder he calls you Uncle Nice," she said; "but you mustn't let him bother you. Don't you think his picking up that name shows he is beginning to think?"

A SLAVE TO DUTY

"Of course I do," laughed Frank; "it shows discernment."

"I like that little chap," said Frank, when Wait had gone; "there *is* a chance for him. Not to be like other boys, poor little defrauded chap, but to be able to do things with his hands so that his life will not be all a burden. One thing anybody must see, he is very sweet-natured."

"That is his mother's gift to him," said Mrs. Wilder.

"Yes, Wait had always the sweetest temper," Nora stuck in, "and she was so unselfish she nearly ruined my disposition. Oh, I mean it, mamma; if I wanted a thing, and two couldn't have it, she would deceive and cudgel her conscience into alleging that she didn't want it at all, and I must have it. Positively, I wonder I am as decent as I am. She had a voracious appetite for self-sacrifice, and I was her victim, because you wouldn't be."

"Her husband didn't object to her self-sacrifice," said Frank. "What a brute he was! Do you remember that night when I happened up suddenly, and she came over with Nora? He had the jimjams and imagined Nora was a devil's child—he was painting some sort of witch picture just then—and wanted to shoot her. Wait insisted on going back herself. So I went with her. He was quiet enough with the doctor and me. I tried my best to get Wait to leave him, then, but she wouldn't. He was her husband; she had promised for better or for worse. There is only one thing that would make it right for her to leave him. 'Well, the whole world knows you've plenty of that,' says I; 'if that's all you're haggling about, come now!' But of course I had nothing but gossip, and she wouldn't believe that. I talked with her half an hour, until she was shivering and blue around the mouth, and I felt like an assassin, but it was no use. She said, 'Oh, Frank, you've been a kind brother to me; I hate to oppose you—'"

"She *did*," cried Mrs. Wilder. "Wait has always thought everything of you, ever since that time Clay ran away with the doctor's phaeton and horse to Maxwell, and you brought it home and wouldn't tell who took it, and were suspended for it."

A SLAVE TO DUTY

"More fool I," said Frank. "I got that sneak safe home to the house, drunk as he was, and got two months off and a rowing from my father, and a letter that was worse than a rowing from my mother, for I know she cried all the way through it. Oh, I owe Clay one for that! But I was telling you what she said. 'I can't desert Clay,' says she; 'he has only me. You think I have no influence over him, because you only see when I fail. You see how unhappy we are sometimes; you don't see our happier times—' I cut in right there. 'Are your happier times happy?' says I. She got tangled up in her conscience directly, and couldn't answer—dodged, and went to talking about how a man of genius couldn't be judged like other men, and how terribly Clay repented, and how he felt that she was the only thing that kept him from despair and suicide. 'Oh, Frank,' she cried, 'his blood will be on my soul if I leave him!' 'Blood nothing,' said I. 'I know Clay's breed; he'd drink himself blind drunk, and then he'd brace up and paint a ripping good picture and get a pot of money for it.' I was right, too, but I couldn't make Wait see it that way. And I suppose I went off crosser than I ever expected to be at Wait. Poor Wait! I begged her for little Nora, but she said he was fond of the child. I told her it wasn't safe. It *wasn't*."

He was talking with vehemence, striding up and down the room before he finished. Mrs. Wilder was brushing away the tears.

"Don't say it, Frank," pleaded she; "you do him injustice. God knows I have no cause to excuse him, but let us be just even to the cruel and unjust. He threw that bust at Wait, not Nora, and it never touched the child. The doctor said it was her heart; that she could not have lived many years in any case. *He* thought that he had killed her, because when she fell she struck her forehead, and the blood was streaming from it. But it was all her heart."

"He frightened her to death instead of hitting her with a wild throw. I don't see it makes things any better for him," retorted Frank, bitterly.

"But, Frank, Wait said he *never* was cruel to little Nora. It was only in his delirium, when he thought she was something else, that he was—was dangerous."

"And how about Wait?" said Frank, between his teeth. "Did he ever strike *her?*"

Mrs. Wilder flushed and shook her head.

"Wait would never tell if he had."

"But you have eyes; what do you think yourself?"

"It may have been; I don't know. Once Wait had a bruise on the side of her cheek. She said it was an accident, and I—I didn't dare to question her, Frank. It seemed to me I couldn't live if he had; and yet I knew she wouldn't leave him, and so I was afraid to know, and didn't question her. You will think I was very pusillanimous and useless all that bad time; but, Frank, I never used to question her about anything. I used to ask about Clay, just as if he were like other husbands, and I kept little Nora here all I could, and did what I could for Wait in little ways."

"How New England!" exclaimed Nora, "*we* would have had it out with Wait, but we didn't half realize it, away off there in Chicago. Clay always kept straight when we made a visit, and Wait kept things so close; but she couldn't keep them from the servants. And then the townspeople talked. They never liked him because he never made no secret how he hated Jeffries' people."

"I remember the reason he gave me for living in Jeffries—so he could leave the dam place oftener," said Frank. "But of course the real reason was that his uncle left him his three thousand a year on condition he lived in Jeffries. Then he owned the house, and it could not be sold during his life. Oh, his uncle was a wise old boy!"

"Didn't he have but three thousand at *any* time, Frank?" Mrs. Wilder questioned. "Why, he had four servants and horses and carriages and those—those people coming to see him. Wait always came over to me when they came. She had such a hard time keeping nice girls; they said they didn't like to have the gentleman of the house swear at them, and," rather dryly, "I fancy they liked less to have him kiss them. When I heard that, I felt it would be right for Wait to leave him. But I couldn't convince her. The bills were a part of the misery. It was so humiliating to have a decent man like Hollin, the butcher, for instance, that we have always dealt with, come up to Wait herself and tell her he wouldn't ask her, but he needed the money to pay his own bills, and he had sent in the bill to Mr. Bostwick so many times; and when she asked him, to find it had been running two years, and was eight hundred dollars! And the others were not quite so bad, but the amounts were larger sometimes."

"What did Wait do?"

"Why, you know he was very generous to her, and gave her beautiful jewels."

"I'm sure that as long as his credit held out he would be the most lavish of men to her—or any other lady."

"That was the trouble, Frank. Wait took a string of pearls he gave her and sold it and paid Hollin; but when she came to try to pay the others, she found that almost all of the things had not been paid for. She returned them all. Then she insisted that they make some kind of arrangement with their creditors, so they could get payments on the debts. That was what made him so furious. Of course, he made a large income by his pictures, but he was so erratic. For a month he would paint night and day, almost; make her fetch him all his meals and wait on him, and then for six months he might not touch a brush. I don't see how he ever accomplished anything. And you know he always had times of going away without notice, and staying a few days or a week. Once he stayed a month, and she was wild with anxiety. That," added Mrs. Wilder, with a touch of unconscious irony, "was during the first year of her marriage; she wasn't so anxious later. She didn't venture to make any search for him, for that threw him into a violent passion; so she would appear as if he were absent quite naturally. She struggled so hard, poor child, to hide things, even from me. It was only after he died that she told me about the debts. That was because she wanted to take the income which was continued to her and the children in case of his death and pay the debts. She took every cent from the sale of the house, and, Frank, that girl hasn't spent a hundred dollars a year on herself since

A SLAVE TO DUTY

Clay ran away and was drowned. Bertie has his own income; she wouldn't stint him."

"Did it ever occur to you, mother," said Frank, by this time back comfortably in the easy-chair, "that there is precious little known about Clay Bostwick's death? He ran out of the house when he found his child was dead, and never was seen again until a dead body in his clothes was fished up in the Charles river. There was nothing except the clothes by which he could be identified, and while perhaps this meant nothing, the body was an inch and a half shorter than Bostwick. Oh, don't look so scared, both of you! I haven't heard anything; I simply spoke out my thoughts. If the cur wasn't dead he would have sneaked back after the money before this. But see here, mother, why wasn't *I* told of Wait's scrimping herself? We've got to stop it, you know. Pay off the proper debts and squelch the others, and generally clear decks."

"If Wait won't let me help her, do you suppose she will let *you?*" Mrs. Wilder asked, with a smile that trod hard on a sigh.

A SLAVE TO DUTY

"Well, hardly; and I dare say I ought to be obliged to her for forgiving me the tremendously plain talk I gave her the last time I advised her to leave Bostwick. It was one time I was here. Whenever I was here, I advised her to throw her husband overboard. The last time I came, she had an errand to Boston, and I didn't see her. But this time I sailed in at such a rate, I didn't dare to tell Nora."

"I've always suspected you said frightful things to her."

"Well, there you all were never mentioning the dog's habits to him or to her, and being as polite to him as if he were a decent man. It kept my temper on the jump, and I determined to have it out with her. He had come home drunk. He never got drunk in an ordinary, respectable way like other people—topple over and put him to bed and wake him up ashamed of himself and wanting a new heart and a new stomach created in him the next morning—not a bit of it. He never got so he couldn't walk straight and talk straight until the very collapse at the end; but his nerves were all flayed alive, as if good whisky were sulphuric acid. But then he drank such grotesque sweet stuffs in his esthetic, tommyrot notions—liqueurs and mixed stuff and sweet champagne, ugh!—I don't wonder he went raving crazy after a week of such insults to his stomach. He came home and told his wife he was tired of seeing that—never mind what he called poor little Bertie! I never saw Wait angry before, but she did fire up at him, then."

"Where were you to hear all this?" exclaimed Nora.

"Outside on the veranda. It was a warm summer night. I innocently walked on the piazza until the maid could tell Mrs. Bostwick I was there. After the maid had gone upstairs, Mr. and Mrs. Bostwick were having it out in the music-room. I caught on to the situation in a flash, and I listened."

"Frank!" Nora said the word, but Mrs. Wilder looked at him.

"That's right," said Frank, tapping his white, square finger-tips together softly. "You must remember I haven't the New England conscience in full bloom; I have only a plain, horse-sense, working, Western conscience that sometimes takes a nap. I wanted to hear, and I listened till things got warm, when I stepped in and offered Bostwick the choice of walking out of the window or being kicked out. He was pretty wiry, but he walked; and then I read the riot act to Wait; I told her she ought to leave that brute—next minute. I told her it wasn't only the dam degradation of the life with him; it was—and then I pointed to Bertie. Yes, I was determined to talk plain, for once. I guess I did. It was a year after I had first begged her to leave Bostwick that Bertie was born. '*That* is a worse crime than any divorce,' said I. But I didn't do any good. She fainted, and I loaded her into a carriage and took her over to you, mother. But it was no use; she went back the next day."

"Oh, Frank, it was harsh, dear, when her whole being is so bound up in that boy! She only did what she thought to be right." His mother-in-law looked at him with a mixture of fright and compulsory condemnation and unwilling, womanly admiration for his daring and his strength. "Yes, you did very wrong, Frank, and I'm thankful Nora has a husband like you," cried Mrs. Wilder.

"And that Wait's husband is dead," added Frank.

"Well, it's good to hear Wait singing as she used to, and running after mother with rubbers—Hullo, here she is back again! Well, young feller!"

But Bertie bounded into the room into Frank's arms, and burst out sobbing; Frank could feel the heart thumping against his bony little chest. "Oh, now, that's not the way to do, young feller!" He soothed the child more by his voice than his words. "What's happened?"

"Bad—man!" gasped Bertie.

"Bad man? What did bad man do to frighten you? Come on, tell us."

Frank, it was noticeable, always talked to Bertie as if he were of the same mental force as other boys, and some obscure nerve in the mother's shamed heart vibrated to the unforced tone. As she watched the man soothe the boy, the lines of her face changed as the lines of a reflected face change in running water.

"Frank," said she, "if there were any danger threatening Bertie, and I couldn't do much for him, would you take him to some good institution and see that he was properly cared for, for awhile?"

Frank's keen eyes narrowed and his mouth set itself in a hair's breadth straighter line.

"Of course I'll look out for the little chap," said he; "but what are you driving at, Wait? Has Bostwick turned up?"

"Yes," said Wait.

Often when a family has, for a long time, dreaded a blow in secret (ever struggling to persuade itself that there is no blow to fall), when the hair snaps and the sword falls, there is a revulsion of frankness; they tell themselves, out loud, that they always expected it.

"I knew he would come!" exclaimed poor Mrs. Wilder. She went to her daughter and began with trembling fingers to remove her cape; it is the instant impulse to treat any afflicted person as helpless. Nora fluttered around her sister and made her sit down. Then she brought a glass of water and a fan, although it was rather a chilly April day and a fire was blazing behind the old-fashioned andirons

Frank, being a man and seeing no chance of service, kept his seat and whispered to Bertie, who suddenly burst out into a cackle of laughter. Bertie's laugh was always unhuman and painful; now it was ghastly.

"You must be mistaken, Wait," said Nora, although a moment before she had echoed her mother's plaint.

"No, I wasn't mistaken, Nora," replied Wait; her voice was like ice. "He had been very ill, he said; and he had for the most of the time been away—in Australia. That was why we had not heard."

"Was he— was he—" Mrs. Wilder stumbled over the word; it seemed a dreadful one to the reticent New England woman.

"He was perfectly sober," said Wait. "He told me he hadn't been drinking for a long time."

"How did he frighten Bertie?" Frank asked.

"I was so startled I screamed; and he held Bertie to—to prevent him running away."

Frank whispered a question in Bertie's ear, to which the child nodded eagerly, beginning to roll up the sleeve of his little velvet blouse; but Frank stopped him with another whisper. "He didn't mean to hurt the child," said Wait, turning her miserable eyes on Frank. "He hasn't the strength. He looked very ill; I never saw him look so ill; and he said that he had only come back to die. He said he wanted to see me, and he asked if he might go to little Nora's grave—"

Nora's disgust overflowed her prudence as the Mississippi races through a broken levee. "The thing that made Clay so *detestable* wasn't his wickedness, but his repentance!" she cried. "He was loathsome, *then!* How did he know he had not killed Nora?"

"I told him."

Mrs. Wilder groaned; she couldn't help it; Nora sprang furiously out of her chair, crying, "You let go the only hold we have on him?"

"I know," Wait answered, meekly. "I seem like a fool to you, Nora, but he asked me, and I had to tell the truth."

A SLAVE TO DUTY

"That depends," muttered Nora, but it was under her breath. She was now pacing the floor, too feverishly excited to keep still like Frank. "I think the best, the very best thing is for you to go away with Frank somewhere, to-night, and leave us to settle with that fellow."

But Wait in her turn rose, not with energy, like her sister, but limply, dragging herself up, and said, "I can't talk until I have thought it over. Bertie, come with mamma."

Bertie shook his head, and murmured, "Uncle Nice." Not until Frank had whispered a sentence to him and slipped his own penknife in his pocket, would he clamber off his refuge and follow his mother. It would have been better for them to talk; and each of them sought in his or her mind for some innocent sentence that Wait might hear without being wounded; but nobody found any, and they sat staring at each other, while the footfalls wearily climbed the stair. Then both women looked at the man, both simultaneously said, "Frank, what shall we do?"

Frank did not give them much comfort. He had pulled out a note-book and pencil. "Is the telegraph office open Sundays?" he said; "and where does the operator live?"

Mrs. Wilder told him.

"Is Dacre still cashier of the bank? And lives at the same place? And does old Squire Barber still deal out justice?"

Mrs. Wilder answered his questions concisely, without return questions, and to his satisfaction, except in the last instance. The old justice was dead.

"Well, never mind; it can't be helped. Keep Wait in the house if you can; and don't expect me back until you see me. Mother, what does Wait mean to do?"

"She means to go back, to Clay, I think, Frank. Do you suppose he really is likely to die?"

"It's possible; he's gone the pace so that his dying is always in the deal; but he's so foxy you can't tell. He'd be a pestiferous invalid, I should say, anyhow. Don't worry; we shan't have to take care of him."

Then he had gone, and the women could only sit and listen, or steal to the stair and

A SLAVE TO DUTY

listen there for some sound behind the closed door at the head.

And Wait kneeled by the bed, while Bertie gurgled happily over his boat, which he had recovered and was stealthily carving.

The attitude was a vague support to her; for she was half fainting with weariness. She tried to think, to consider; but instead of definite arguments, or even definite temptations, her married life floated vaguely before her in detached scenes. She was hearing Frank's impatient voice, "I tell you, you go back to a life of *infamy!* That man's marriage was a crime. His father had insane streaks; he himself is the worst kind of an insane man—a willfully vicious one! You don't know half how bad he is!" Didn't she? Yet there were scenes that seemed burned into her heart with red-hot iron, so that the touch of the lightest memory on them made her writhe and moan in torment. "The dam degradation of it!" It was cruel in Frank to say that. Didn't he know she was his wife, Clay's wife! She could see the nurse's oblong face and the two double chins and the flap of flannel over the baby's head. But the baby was all right. Not a pretty baby, her poor little boy; but all right. And she would not believe that he must be like his father. God would be merciful. Anything! anything rather than that! And perhaps God had been merciful, in this strange, distorted way. Her baby was safe. He would always need her, always be her baby. She turned her body, still on her knees, to look for Bertie, and saw him with his boat. He put it hastily behind his back, and in so doing cut his hand slightly with the knife. The sight of the blood put the half-distracted woman into a passion of anguish. She clasped him frantically to her heart, in a clasp so tight that he was scared.

"Hu't! hu't!" he whimpered, using one of his few words, and rubbing his arm. She pulled up his sleeve. There were the livid marks of fingers on the white, soft flesh. Her kisses and her tears rained down on it. "I can't take him, I can't take him with me," she would cry. And then, "Cruel! he was *always* cruel!" But in a very little while, bending over to help her dizzy way across the floor, she knelt again; and again the squalid procession of her sufferings and her struggles drifted to the accompaniment of her prayers for light.

She tried to recall those earlier days when she had felt the charm that many a woman found in Clay Bostwick. He was a mere stripling. They were only children when they were married. Her mother had feared. Even then there were ugly rumors and stories buzzing about. Nora would fetch them home and beg her mother to send Clay away; he was not a nice boy. But Clay, when her mother talked to him with pretense of severity and inward compassion for the delicate young lad—Clay had burst into tears and admitted he wasn't what he ought to be, but—if she would only let him stay, only try him once more! He had no mother, and his father was worse than none. And Mrs. Wilder had relented. He had stayed. How attentive he was; how he worked over the only thing he cared for, art! Yet—how could they tell, those unworldly, kindly women, what those occasional absences of his meant? Even now, Wait wondered, did she comprehend *all* that they meant? And the years in Paris, when the letters came at intervals, and beautiful gifts for her mother—she was glad her mother would not take them—and then the handsome young fellow with his halo of success about him, and the notices of the picture in the salon, and the intoxicating prophecies—was it so wrong and strange that they who did not know the world, should believe in him, that Wait should love him? "Waitstill, my own little Waitstill, it's the sweetest name in the world, the dear little Puritan name," he had murmured, "and I have kept it in my heart." His uncle had pushed the marriage. He was sure with Wait the boy would be steady. He knew better before he died.

The procession drifted on. Is there any awakening so cruel as the slow, then faster, then hideously swift awakening of a wife to a knowledge of the real nature of marriage with a man whose surface refinement, by its greater power of imagination, only stimulates and expands his vices!

There was not a clean, robust, honest ideal of her childhood that her husband did not outrage by his speech and his actions. He was without truth or honor or temperance or purity or any faithfulness. His first passion waned before she had worn out her pretty bridal clothes. It would return in the shape in which such a feeling does return to such a man; but it was never strong enough, after the first, to hold his bitter tongue, nor to curb a single brutal whim, far less to cleanse his life. Wait was like the daintily kept, warm, lighted home that was always ready for him. When he had chased the excitement for which his abused nerves were crying, through vice into satiety and disgust and despair, there was Wait always ready to nurse him back to health. She never upbraided him, she never sniveled over him; in truth, she never said anything about his "ways." He liked that. On the whole he had liked Wait. Wait found herself pushing *his* point of view and *his* words themselves into the foreground of her consciousness, and trying to understand him, as an outsider who knew the world would understand him—as Frank would, for instance.

"Wait, I'm played out. I'm out of the

scheme. All I want is a decent place to crawl into and be safe, where I can see you. Repent! *You* never talked repent before. When I finished a spree and was sick you amused me, and never mentioned. That's the kind of wife for me. Wait, I can paint a great picture still, if you'll only keep me straight for six months—and I live that long. Wait, send that jabbering creature off a little, so I can see you. Great—oh, no, I'm not going to swear; I was only going to pay you a compliment on your looks. I did love you, little sweetheart. I never loved any other woman. You might take that into account about forgiving me. And if suffering counts, the hell I went through after—" It was real, his shudder. It was real, too, the pallor of his haggard face and the glassy look of his beautiful violet eyes, as he pleaded with her that afternoon. The one plea that overquelled everything was his dreary iteration. "Wait, I haven't *anybody* but you! Wait, save me; let me die half-way decent!"

She was not afraid of his cruelty; she was afraid, with a terror of fear, of his reviving tenderness. "I never can love him," she groaned. "To-day, I thought how horrid he looked; and his hand—I wanted to scream when he touched me. And he is my husband!" She began to pray in a whisper, not in sentences that she shaped to hold her own sore need, but in collects or prayers from the litany or bits of childish verse, in anything that might distract her mind from the visions that cursed her.

It was at this moment that Mrs. Wilder crept half-way along the hall and caught a murmur, "cleanse the desires of our hearts," and crept away again.

"She's praying, Nora," she whispered. "Oh, child, surely if she prays only for light, not to be happy or be saved, God will. He *must* hear and enlighten her!"

"I'm not so sure, mamma," said Nora, stolidly. "How is it that the Protestants prayed and the Catholics prayed, and then they got up from their knees and burned and beheaded each other for the glory of God? And besides, I'm not so sure we don't make up our minds first, and then pray to have them strengthened!"

"But if we are acting against our own happiness—"

"Mamma, I think there are lots of people who are sure anything that hurts them must be right. Sometimes I think it is our *duty* to be happy. And another thing that rouses me almost to madness in pious people, is that they usually pick out some worthless, selfish object to sacrifice themselves to, and to sacrifice all their friends and relations with them, without a quaver! Now, if Wait wants to sacrifice herself, that's one thing; but dumping us beside her on the altar, that's another."

Her mother sighed heavily, and slipped out of the room.

Nora, in a fever of impatience, was perforce left to pound "Rise crowned with light," to the air of the Russian national hymn, as the most powerful and yet proper Sunday music left her.

Mrs. Wilder came down, looking as if she had been crying.

"I can see Wait and you are agreed, mamma"—Nora ran into the fray at once—"well, what is it?"

A SLAVE TO DUTY

"She feels that she must go back to him, Nora. He is her husband, and she promised for better, for worse, you know; and then she feels that he is not going to live long; and she can't thrust a helpless, maybe dying man aside. So—she is going to find him and fetch him here!"

"*What!*" screamed Nora.

"I know what Frank will say, Nora," said Mrs. Wilder, sinking into a chair, "but I can't have Wait away, exposed to I don't know what miseries; and if he is in the house he will be under some restraint—a little, anyway. If Frank and you will take Bertie—"

"Do you suppose Frank will stay in this house one minute after that villain is here?"

Mrs. Wilder began to cry. But Nora raged on: "Of course, you haven't thought of *yourself;* how Clay's habits will turn the house upside down! Betty will give warning, and I don't blame her; and Frank said he never knew any cook to roast ducks better than she does, or to so invariably make lovely bread; she's got all the old recipes that we used to like; and lots of good new things; and she's so used to your ways, it will be like an earthquake to have her go; and she'll take Liza, she'll never let that young thing stay in a house where Clay Bostwick is—"

"But you forget how ill he is; he's going to die."

"He isn't!" declared Nora, furiously. "He'll outlive us all; and if he does die, he'll contrive to run us all off our feet before the Lord takes mercy on us. I saw Clay Bostwick once when he was having a fit of sickness. The whole house was upset, and poor Wait didn't get a moment day nor night, except when he was asleep. A selfisher brute I never knew; and I felt as if, were I alone with him, I should be tempted to skip all his medicines, in hopes it would kill him. I tell you, mamma, you and Wait will make a murderer out of me before you get done. You shan't have him in the house; I'll—I'll burn it down first!"

"Would you have me let Wait go away, with narrow means and this sick man to care for, and their house sold? Wait talked of

A SLAVE TO DUTY

going to the hotel to-night, and maybe renting the Norris house to-morrow—"

"That tumble-down shanty!"

"I couldn't have them go there. I know Clay couldn't bear it; and I told Wait I should appeal to him if she insisted. And think how people would talk!"

Nora gave a cynical snort of laughter. "I believe, mamma, you would think of that if you were dying. Dying! How do I know Clay may not go raving crazy, and kill you or Wait? He isn't safe!"

"Nora, Wait said, 'We can't do anything but put our trust in God; though He slay me, yet will I trust Him!' If Wait is doing what she thinks is right, God will not permit—"

"God permitted Bertie," said Nora, solemnly.

Mrs. Wilder had no answer; she looked piteously at her younger daughter, who seemed changed, all the gay lightness of her nature vanished.

"Frank is right," Nora went on. "We dare not assume that we are obeying God when we are wronging our fellow-beings.

A SLAVE TO DUTY

A woman may have a right to sacrifice her own life; she has no right to sacrifice the lives of her possible children. Bertie's existence is a crime. It is a crime for Wait to return to that man now, and abandon Bertie."

"But where is the way out?" cried Mrs. Wilder.

"Frank will find it," said Nora, confidently.

At this moment she saw Frank at the gate, and sank back in her chair with the breathless sensation that comes when one perceives a crisis approach.

Frank opened the door and nodded smilingly.

"Frank, Wait wants to go back to him," cried Nora, "and mamma insists that they shall come here!"

"Whew!" puffed Frank, "I'm out of breath. Well, I guess Wait will have a time finding him, that's all. Can't any one get a hard working and walking man a glass of cool beer or lemonade, or something?"

Mrs. Wilder rose, but Nora pushed her into a chair. "I'll get him a glass of water;

that's quite enough until he has told us. Frank, tell us this minute, where's that man?"

"More than I know, my dear; running still, maybe. Where's Wait?"

"Up-stairs."

"Tell her to come down. No, I'll call up to her; I'll see her, myself."

They heard him run lightly up the stairs and rap on the door. Then he ran into the room. After awhile they heard him coming down the stairs. He held Bertie in his arms; his face was stern.

"Wait has taken matters into her own hands," said he. "She has gone. This is a note from her."

He handed the slip of paper to Mrs. Wilder, whose trembling fingers could not unfold it; she gave it to Nora. Nora read it aloud:

"I cannot sacrifice you, too. I am going to Clay. I must. God will help me do my duty."

The Jeffries station was built before the days of fanciful architecture and parterres and flower-beds. It was a dingy barn of a place, a vast blackened roof above the double tracks which shone like silver. On either side, was a platform where the trains halted, a mere breathing-space, and passengers, previously warned by the agent, made a frantic rush to clamber on the steps. There was a kind of cage for the ticket-agent, a dismal baggage-room, and a more dismal waiting-room. Week-days the waiting-room usually had a tenant, for the town is near enough to Boston to have a continual rumbling of trains; but Sunday afternoon there are only two trains to Boston direct, and these in this staid little village are scantily patronized. Only one man, Frank Mallory, walked up and down the platform waiting for some one or something this Sunday afternoon. The agent knew him, of course, and watched him with the hungry curiosity of an active man with leisure on his hands. Presently, Rufus Swift, who used to be constable, but was now a private detective in Boston, wafts of whose fame drifted occasionally to Jeffries, walked briskly on to the platform. The agent knew that Swift had come up from Boston two hours previous. And he wondered the more "what that rich Chicago feller wanted with Rufe."

His interest could not make him hear the conversation, however. It was brief.

"Did you find her?" said Frank.

"No, Mr. Mallory. I think she had been to the house, for I found that the chairs were moved and one drawer in that table pulled out. It is clear he had appointed that little deserted summer-house as a meeting-place. And she had kept the appointment; but she was gone."

"Could he possibly have got any word to her after he left us?"

"Well, he might write a note on the train, and send it back by some one. He had plenty of money," with a grim smile, "to pay a messenger. And he might do it—just out of meanness, to spite you."

"In that case—which is quite possible—what would he be likely to ask of her? To join him, I suppose."

"That's how it strikes me, too."

"It is half-past six. If she wants to go to-night, she would try for this train, don't you think?"

A SLAVE TO DUTY

"I do think, sir—and there she comes down the hill! I can see her coming down the hill. If we stand up close to the door she can't see us, not till she steps out on the platform."

"She's left herself ten minutes. She means to go." As he spoke, Frank flattened his big person against the wall of the waiting-room, outside, and Swift followed his example. They did not have long to wait. There was a light footstep, a rustle of skirts, and Mrs. Bostwick stepped out of the door. Frank laid his hand on her arm.

"Don't scream, Wait," said he, smiling. "The agent is here, and he might hear you."

Wait did not scream, but she turned very pale. "Do you need to make it so hard for me, Frank?"

"Of course. I'm not doing this for fun, dear. If you'll take my arm and walk with me I'll explain the whole affair."

"I'd rather stay here, Frank."

"As you please. Don't go, Swift. You remember Mr. Rufus Swift, Wait?"

Even in the strain of the moment Wait did not forget her sweet courtesy; she held

A SLAVE TO DUTY

out her hand to Rufus, saying with a tremulous smile, "I hope your mother is well. We have heard of your success in the papers."

"Mother's well," returned Rufus, bowing, and with a wrath at Bostwick struggling with a sense of delight at her remembering his "success" at such a time.

"Swift came up here in answer to a telegram," said Frank. "Will you walk a little with me?"

This time Wait did not refuse. He walked as he spoke, not looking at her.

"Let us cut this short, Wait. You mean to go to Boston to join Bostwick. *Well, you can't do it.* Shall I tell you why?"

"I must do it, Frank; please don't make it so hard for me!"

He patted the hand on his arm with a brusque tenderness. "How you tremble, poor child! I believe you think I am going to hold you by force. I would if there were any need of it. But there isn't. You will not want to go after you hear what I am going to tell you. That is, simply that your going would ruin Bostwick. It would, because Swift and I would go, too, and follow you, and arrest Bostwick."

"It wasn't murder; you can't make it out murder—"

"We don't need to try. We couldn't, at best, get more than a manslaughter verdict, and we have something else. Please turn. We shall arrest Clay Bostwick for stealing two thousand dollars from me to-day. We have plenty of evidence on that. Swift saw him take it."

Wait turned a strange entreaty up at his face. "You are not telling me—"

"Here is Swift," said Frank, coolly. "Swift, is it true that Mr. Bostwick stole two thousand dollars of me in the summer-house at the Norris Place—took it out of my coat?"

"Yes, sir, it is true. I'll go before any court in the land and swear it," said Swift.

"If you will walk a little way with me, I'll explain," said Frank, gently; "or shall we sit on this bench?" He sat down beside her and in an even voice told his tale.

"Of course, I had no idea of letting Bostwick carry you off. So I telegraphed to

A SLAVE TO DUTY

Swift. He luckily had been engaged on some business of mine, and came up at a moment's notice. I wanted him because Bostwick would remember him as the constable, and might not know of Swift's new pursuits. I had him rig up with a star. It was easy enough to run Bostwick down; and when I dropped a hint that I intended to run him out of town, I knew I could count on every man, woman and child in Jeffries helping me."

"But why—they don't know—" The words faltered on Wait's lips.

"Don't deceive yourself, Wait," said Frank, gravely. "This is a New England village, where they not only know how to use their eyes, but know how to seem not to see. They know everything. Everything, Wait. They have for a long time. So instead of your coming to meet him, I came; and I assure you he wasn't a little bit glad to see me, either. I spoke to him fair enough, at first. I told him I was willing to pay him spot cash to leave, and I took out the money that I had had the cashier get me from the bank—taking down the number of the notes, by the way. I showed him I could pay him if he would once for all clear out, go to Australia, or anywhere that was far enough. I admit that I wasn't mealy-mouthed about it, and let him see that I though him a hound. He flew into a passion. Then I whistled, and Swift appeared and arrested him for murder. He tried to brazen it out, and fell back on what you had told him. 'We'll *try* whether that is right,' says I. 'We're sure of manslaughter, anyhow, and that will keep you in prison long enough to kill you, with your weak lungs—'"

"Oh, Frank, that was—"

"Brutal, wasn't it? It had a purpose; to frighten him. And it succeeded. He said he would write a note to you, telling you that he would never come back, and releasing you entirely. He said (with a sort of leer) that he could write something that would make you willing to give him up. So I threw my coat down on the bench and was bending over him, watching him, when we heard a scream, and then another, coming up from that pond; a woman's screams that her baby would drown. I called to

Swift to run to see, while I guarded the door. The screams kept up, and I ran a little way—just a few steps to see, you know, what was going on. But that was enough for him. He was off, out the other door with my pocketbook."

"But the woman—the baby?"

"Oh, the baby was all right. The woman was all right."

Wait whirled on her seat, and her eyes dove into the evasive eyes of her brother-in law. "Frank, why didn't *you* run out, leaving Swift?"

"I—I wanted to guard Bostwick."

"But you didn't guard him!"

"Very well, perhaps it is better to give you the truth straight. I wanted to have the proof if Bostwick stole that money. I have it."

"Frank, was there any woman or any baby in the water, at all?"

Frank shrugged his shoulders. "You see what you drive a poor well-meaning Western brother-in-law into, Wait, with your slavish notions of duty. I have to pass off a bogus policeman, which is undoubtedly against the law, and I have to tempt a rascal into theft;

now don't you think you have made enough occasion for me to sin? and instead of throwing your own happiness and ours away to save that fellow, suppose you let up a little and let *me* save my soul! For I tell you, if you follow that man, I will follow him, too, and I'll send him to the penitentiary. I can and I will. You can be sure he'll not thank you for following him, if it comes to that. Wait, are you ready to come home?"

The roar of the approaching train filled the air. His hand was on her arm.

"Would you disgrace us all by doing such an awful thing?" she breathed, faintly. "Am I not unhappy enough without that brand—and Bertie—"

"If I can't save you without sending that brute to the pen, I'll send him. And I'll send him to the gallows just as readily. As to Bertie, the best thing in the world for him is to have his father utterly effaced. Did you see his arm?"

Wait turned away. The train creaked and groaned and tore out of the station. The telegraph wires whined overhead under the lash of its wind.

A SLAVE TO DUTY

"*Let* yourself be saved, Wait," said Frank, passing his arm about her. "Dear little sister, there is no other way, for *I* won't let you be lost!"

The village coach was waiting. The agent related to his eager listeners that there was nothing different that he could see in the way Mrs. Bostwick looked; she just walked to the coach with Mr. Mallory, and Mallory gave the boy a dollar for coming down so quick—and that was the only queer thing he saw happen. As for Mr. Swift, he went on to Boston.

A day later, however, the village had another sensation. Wait had submitted to be put to bed. She had sobbed on her mother's shoulder, and confessed the relief that she could not resist; and Mrs. Wilder had heard the story and sighed to Frank, "I know you are acting wrong, Frank, but I can't help being glad you were here!" Wait was up-stairs now, and the household had subsided into its customary decorous quiet. Betty and Liza were washing the early dinner dishes in a pleasantly excited frame of mind. Nora sat in the little parlor with

A SLAVE TO DUTY

Bertie and Frank. Frank was smoking. Bertie, as usual, nestled close to him, whittling at his boat. All at once, Bertie glanced up and sank back with a cry of fright. Nora lifted her eyes; she sprang to her feet.

"Frank," she gasped, "it's Clay!"

Frank, too, rose; and as he rose the door opened, and not waiting for a ring, but quite as in the times when he was living in the town, Clay Bostwick walked into the room. Behind him came Mrs. Wilder, white and trembling.

"It's you, is it?" said Frank. Then he beckoned to Mrs. Wilder. Any one could hear his undertone. "Mother, please telephone for a policeman and Squire Keats—"

"Stop," said Bostwick's soft, cleanly modulated tones—he had a beautiful voice—"stop; after you have heard what I have come to say, perhaps you won't care to call the police in to help in the family wash!"

"I have no objection to hearing you," said Frank. Nora slipped out of the room.

"First, why didn't Wait come to Boston, as I sent her word?"

"Wait has had better council than yours,"

said Frank. "Wait's done with you. Is that all you have to say why you shan't be arrested for stealing?"

"Not near—But I wish you'd get me a glass of wine or something—this is a frightful climate; I always hated it." He sat down on the sofa and leaned back his head. He did look ill and haggard. But, as Mrs. Wilder instantly saw, he was dressed in his old lavish style; his check tweed was new and of the latest cut. There was a perfectly fitting glove on one hand, and on the other sparkled a diamond ring.

How strange is the power of custom! This man had brought her the most cruel grief of her life. If so mild a soul could hate, she hated Clay Bostwick; yet when she saw him leaning back on her sofa, just as he used to lean when he was in the house, addressing her in the old, familiar, petulant, appealing tone, she could not resist the impulse to serve him in the old fashion. "You'll do better without wine, Clay," she answered, "but I'll bring you a cup of hot coffee."

He smiled. "You always were a dear,

and you made the best coffee in the world. Yes, do fetch me some."

"Well," said Frank—Mrs. Wilder had pattered out of the room—"well, come to the point! What do you want?"

"I want that two thousand," said Clay, pleasantly.

"What will you give for it? You know I can send you to the penitentiary. It was grand larceny."

"Oh, drop that, you don't want to send me to the penitentiary. And you know Wait has been using my money for two years; and she has sold the house—where's that money?"

"You can have a lawyer inquire. You will have plenty of leisure, for I'm going to telephone, now. That was my money you took, and not Wait's—"

"But see here; don't get up. I want that money and—I don't want Wait! *Now*, will you sit down and listen to me?"

"You were of another mind, yesterday."

"I was ill, yesterday; beastly ill; thought I was going to die. Quarreled—never mind, I came out here on an impulse. You danced your cursed money before my eyes, and I had the impulse to teach you a lesson. I swiped it and made off. On the train I sent a message to Wait. She was going to meet me in the summer-house. I sent the message there. Told her to join me in Boston. She wouldn't. Very well, there are others! I thought to myself, 'What a fool you are! that Chicago pig wouldn't mind sending you to prison—'"

"Not a rap," interrupted Frank. "You read me correctly."

"Wait wouldn't come to me when I needed her. All right, I don't care; she's a tedious, mewling prig, anyhow. Say, what do you say to letting me go if I'll give you a confession that I won't have Wait, and want her to get a divorce? I do. I can marry—there's the coffee."

He drank the coffee, and thanked Mrs. Wilder. Then, disregarding her presence, he looked up at Frank. "How's that?"

"I can assure you Wait doesn't want anything to do with you, now or ever," said Frank. "She loathes you. And at the same time she does not want to touch your money. So soon as your creditors are paid—and that will be pretty soon, for the house and furniture all went to them—so soon as that, two thousand a year will be paid to an Australian banking-house to you, in person. Kindly notice the last words. They mean you have to go for things yourself—or send a physician's certificate. You'll sign the papers I have drawn up and had ready for you if you ever turned up."

He drew something out of his pocket and spread the paper on the table. "It's that or the constable," said he.

Clay signed without a word. In turn, he pushed a little bundle over to Frank. "That will give Wait her divorce any time," he sneered. "I'll bid you good-morning. And you, Mrs. Wilder." He made a barely perceptible pause to look at her, before he said, "I don't suppose you'll have very pleasant memories of me; but you *were* good to me, and I know you're a good woman. So's Wait. She was too good. If she had been a little less submissive it would have been better for both of us." He took a step toward the door, but midway paused again,

A SLAVE TO DUTY

this time before Bertie, who had cowered against Frank, not making a sound. "I always hated him," he said to Frank. "You can guess why." Frank nodded. "Poor beggar, you've a hard row before you, and that's a fact. Here, it's a pity you shouldn't have one present from your dad. Catch!" The diamond blazed as it whirled and circled through the air. Bertie caught it, and his heavy face reddened with pleasure.

Clay looked at him; and suddenly in one of the quick revulsions of his unstable temperament, his fine blue eyes filled with tears. He shook the hair from his brow and laughed bitterly. "If I send you a picture will you buy it at a fair price?" he asked Frank.

"If it is a good one, and I like it," said Frank.

He laughed again, and stepped lightly out of the room. They saw him for a second, as he passed the house. They never saw him again.

Mrs. Wilder drew a long sigh. "Poor Clay," she said.

"And will Wait say the same?" said Frank, a little puzzled, not quite pleased.

"I don't know. Yes. But we shall both be thankful. Oh, Frank, what should we have done without you?"

"In spite of my lack of principle?"

"I am afraid," said Mrs. Wilder, "it's awful to think of it that a lack of principle should be so helpful—but perhaps it was ordered that so we should be saved."

"It might be a good thing if more slaves to duty had their chains broken by force," said Frank. "Where's Wait."

Wait sat at her window. She had seen Clay come in; she saw him go out. As his hand was on the gate he turned his head and met her eyes. Something in them, appealing, solemn, held his own gaze a moment. Then, without speaking, he lifted his hat, as he might have lifted it at a funeral, bowed, and turned away.

She watched him out of sight. Then she kneeled down as she had kneeled the day before—but with what different thoughts in her heart!

Nora, outside, softly turned a key in the lock, took it out and stole away, smiling.

A Colonial Dame

THE Bowler block fronted a side street down-town. There was a bakery in the lower story, right-hand corner, and the baker's family lived above. Two dressmakers, a dyer and a seamstress occupied the other rooms in the two stories over the bakery.

The bakery had a local renown for its cream puffs and a very white, delicious bread, the secret of which the baker guarded vigilantly. When any of the people of the town gave large companies, the bread for sandwiches (which, as every one knows, forms an important part of "party refreshments" in a provincial town) was always bought from Brandt. He had a neat slicing machine that saved the hostess no end of trouble. Besides the bread and fancy cakes, he was the author of a very respectable pâté, the contents of which could be varied at will.

A COLONIAL DAME

The Cravens were valued customers of Brandt's, and the Craven carriage was a frequent sight in the street. But Mrs. Craven came oftener to see her old friend on the third floor than to buy of the baker.

One day last June, when the smell of violets and heliotrope was in the air, from Miss Arnold's little window garden, the Craven horses jingled their silver chains before the curbstone, and a comely, stout lady followed a slender young girl from the landau. The young girl stepped back into the carriage, but the stout lady crossed to a side door and toiled up the narrow inside stairs.

"Mrs. Craven is calling on Miss Arnold," said the neighbors. Miss Arnold (Miss Jerusha W. Arnold, read the card on her hall door) was a seamstress. She could build gowns, also; but while her needlework was exquisite, her critics said that she had no ideas. She did not "keep up with the styles," and more enterprising or more pretentious dressmakers left her behind. But she retained a sound clientage of a few wealthy families, where she had her regular

A COLONIAL DAME

engagements for spring and autumn; and there was, besides, a modest little property which had been judiciously invested by the "Craven boys," and Miss Arnold was esteemed a wealthy lady, in the block.

The Cravens (who were very great people in the town) were not only friends; there was, so the gossips related, a second or third cousinship. In fact, Mrs. Craven always spoke of her as "Cousin Jerry." The children had used so to address her. They might address her so now, but they had ceased to speak of her as "Cousin Jerry." Mrs. Craven, however, kept up the intimacy of her girlhood. I suppose it is no secret that the before-mentioned property was a bequest of Mr. Craven; at least, he told Mrs. Craven that he wanted her to remember Jerry, and Mrs. Craven had remembered Jerry liberally. Therefore, the stairs were no new journey to Mrs. Craven. To-day, however, she struggled up them with an unusual expression of anxiety and distress on her kind face.

"I know it'll slip out some way," she panted, "and I don't know but I'd ruther it would. Oh, I wish their father was alive; he wouldn't let the girls do so, I know."

The speech ended in a heavy sigh and a rap on Miss Arnold's door. Instantly it was opened by the seamstress herself. She looked like a caricature of a New England spinster, being very tall, very thin, very straight and very plain. It was a question whether her Roman nose, her prominent teeth, or a slight cast in her left eye ought to have the most credit for this plainness. Plain—singularly, even grotesquely plain—she certainly was; yet to her old friend Ellen Craven's eyes she was attractive. Her hair was thin and straight and gray, but it was silky fine, her skin was delicately fair, and the large teeth were flashing white.

"Why, land's sake, Ellie! is it you?" she exclaimed, as she drew Mrs. Craven into the parlor and the coolest rattan chair. It was a tiny little parlor, the furniture of which tried the taste of the Craven girls, but which, when they were children, they had dearly loved. There was an old-fashioned black haircloth sofa that Miss Arnold's mother had when she was married. There was a

A COLONIAL DAME

rosewood cabinet with shells and ivory boxes and sandalwood and stuffed birds, that an old uncle had brought back from over the seas. And in the center of the room stood the marble-topped table that held a plush photograph album, N. P. Willis' poems in red and gilt morocco, and a small crayon portrait of a young soldier in the clumsy private's blouse and huge trousers of the early sixties. The children used to view this photograph with awe, and be told that it was the picture of a brave man who had died for his country. After a while their mother told them that it was Cousin Jerry's betrothed. She called him "Cousin Jerry's beau," because she was not a person of elegant education like her daughters. The picture faced Mrs. Craven as she sat opposite the table fanning herself with a paper pattern conveniently near. It seemed to her that the dead soldier reproached her. She shifted her position.

"Why, you're all beat out, Ellie!" said Miss Arnold, tenderly.

Now that Timothy Craven was dead, she was the only person in the world who called

Mrs. Craven "Ellie." The Craven girls winced at the diminutive, which truly did not seem appropriate to Mrs. Craven's presence. Ellen, the older girl, said that it was "ridiculous." But Mrs. Craven never heard it without a moving of the heart. It affected her painfully to-day.

"You've been working too hard, that's what's the matter, gittin' ready for Gertie's young man. I hear he's coming to-morrow. I'm so anxious to see him!"

"He ain't going to stay very long," said Mrs. Craven.

"He'll stay to the party, won't he?"

Mrs. Craven's blushes came readily still, in spite of her fifty-odd years. She flushed now, and conscious that her color was heightened, fanned more rapidly. Miss Arnold was eyeing her with a keenness not to be expected of her mild visage and almost timid demeanor; but under her shyness Jerusha Arnold concealed, or rather, it would be fairer to say contained (since she was not conscious of any disguisement) a very shrewd gift of observation. And she had not sewed in private families, and often seen the feet of the skeleton when the closet door was ajar, without picking up some worldly wisdom.

"I suppose you heard from Mrs Brandt about the party," said Mrs. Craven, holding the paper pattern higher. "No, I don't need a fan, Jerry. It ain't much of a party —a lawn party, the girls call it. For Tim's wife. She'll find it pleasanter, being introduced to a good many at once. And I feel grateful to her, being willing to live here after all the attention she's had."

"But Tim's business is here. She don't expect you to move the factory to Chicago or Boston, so's she can go to parties, does she?"

"Of course not; but I'm afraid she'll feel the change. Coming West, too!"

"I guess we won't eat her! But there, I don't show any justice to the girl. She's pretty as a picture, riding by in Tim's new surrey; but I did expect to see more of Tim's wife than jest riding by in her carriage. And I did feel awful cut up, and that's the fact, when I gave up an afternoon only to go and call on her, and a mincing little girl with a cap, told me that Mrs. Craven was very much engaged, and begged to be excused."

"It was her Dante lesson; she never lets anything interrupt that, and the girl said the same to everybody."

"I guess it won't kill me, but it—it hurts, Ellie, to have Tim's wife making a stranger of me. There, I feel better, now I have talked it out! But I hope Gertie's young man will not be so proud. I haven't really had a chance to talk with Gertie since she came back from the East, engaged to him. I can't quite realize it, our Gertie being engaged to be married. He's a fine-appearing young man—in his picture she showed me."

Mrs. Craven considered Reginald rather plain, although she stood in awe of him because Mrs. Tim mentioned him with respect. "He's considerable freckled," she answered, dubiously, "and his nose being broken at football makes his face not so—well, not exactly handsome; but he's of fine family, connected with the Winthrops. Hazel's his cousin. Johnny says he's a very nice fellow, with no nonsense about him. He was at Harvard with Johnny, only in a higher class, of course. He's very s—clever."

"Oh, you can call it smart when you're with *me*, Ellie," said Miss Arnold, dryly; "I don't see why it ain't just as good a word. Well, I hope he'll make Gertie happy, that's all; and I guess he will. I suppose they—they're very much in love?"

Mrs. Craven nodded and sighed.

"Well, we know what it is, Ellie; we've had our day," said the other elderly woman. And she leaned over and gently patted Mrs. Craven's gloved hand. The tears rose to the matron's eyes. "There, there, Ellie! I'm a fool, making you feel bad! Let's talk about the party. Shan't I come and fix the flowers?"

Miss Arnold had a gift for plants. Plain and simple as she seemed, her floral effects showed a magic touch envied by professional florists. Yet the offer brought another and a deeper flush to her friend's kind, anxious face.

"You're just as good as you can be, Jerry," she cried, affectionately, "but I'm ashamed to ask you, for—for the invitations ain't very general, and—and—"

A COLONIAL DAME

"And you ain't going to invite *me*, you mean?" said Miss Arnold, quietly, but her own color had turned.

The tears in Mrs. Craven's eyes rolled down her cheeks; she choked, trying to answer. Suddenly, Miss Arnold put one arm protectingly around the palpitating, plump shoulder.

"There, Ellie, don't go to feeling bad; *I* know you want me; only tell me one thing, was—was it Gertie that asked you not to have me?"

"No, it wasn't," Mrs. Craven cried, regaining a little voice; "it was Tim's wife. She—of course, she doesn't know you, dear, and she has so many social prejudices." A queer smile stole over Miss Arnold's face while Mrs. Craven continued: "She comes of a high family, you know, and she thinks so much of being a gentlewoman, as she calls it, and she's a Colonial Dame, and so I guess she thinks she has to be particular. I told her how we'd been bosom friends for thirty years, and no sister could be kinder or more devoted; but she didn't understand. And afterward, when I talked to the girls, they said they knew Hazel would never get over it. She's New England, and hoards up things. And though they felt awful not to ask you (Miss Arnold's lip curled a little, bitterly), Ellen thought we ought to humor Tim's wife, who is strange, and I guess awful homesick, and—well, I gave in, Jerry; I couldn't bear to contrary Ellen, and Tim's wife, too."

"Never you mind, never you mind, Ellie; I know we love each other, and you don't need to be afraid I'll shame you before your grand friends. I'll come and fix the flowers for you, and then I'll go home."

"And you'll come up to dinner to-morrow, Jerry," pleaded Mrs. Craven.

"I guess not, to-morrow; I've got a good many things on hand."

Mrs. Craven begged in vain; this one little solace of a wounded spirit Miss Arnold could not deny herself. Finally Mrs. Craven left her, comforted, but still heavy-hearted. And after she had gone, the seamstress sat down and cried.

The humblest of us have our little audience, whose approbation is as the breath of our nostrils. Miss Jerry had lived in the block for ten years; they all knew her—her punctual payments and her charities, which were not small, either, in comparison to her income, or in the eyes of the recipients. The Craven friendship was her mark of distinction with her neighbors. She was a great personage to them, although she might be only Miss Arnold, the seamstress, to the town in general. When she donned her one black silk, rich and good, the gift of Mrs. Craven, and pinned on a bit of real lace, from Ellen, with the pretty brooch that Gertie gave her, and the Craven carriage was sent to convey her to a Craven function, the building was agitated; the tenants all felt that they were touching the edge of fashion. They talked about it to their neighbors, and Mrs. Brandt, the baker's wife, always came up next evening, when Miss Arnold returned from her day's work, with a steaming cup of coffee and some fresh rolls hot from the oven, to learn the details of the toilets, and how Brandt's own contributions to the menu were received.

Now, poor Miss Arnold could not but

imagine the questions, "I suppose you are going to the Cravens' great party? No? Why not?" And Jerusha Arnold, who came of Puritan stock, could not find it in her conscience to utter a falsehood. With a corroded heart she would have to answer that she had not received an invitation; further—but her imagination recoiled. Not only was her harmless vanity wounded, but her tears welled from a deeper source. The awkward soldier on the table was Miss Jerry's only lover, and Ellen Craven was her only dear friend. They had been friends for so many, many years; two little girls in school, two apprentices in the dress-making shop, now two women growing old. Both had been orphans.

In the early days Jerusha was the stronger of the two. They opened a little shop together, and it was then that the young superintendent of the wagon works met and loved pretty Ellen Pratt. He married her, and he never regretted his choice of a wife, although, perhaps, as his wealth and importance grew, other people wondered a little that he had not married a woman of wider education. But Ellen Craven was of so gentle, sunny, unselfish a disposition that every one, even her own highly educated children, forgave her the lapses of her tongue and manner.

Certainly Timothy Craven was not the man to undervalue his wife's good qualities. He laughed at her humility and her painstaking, futile efforts to raise the girls' standard. When he discovered her secretly taking Delsarte lessons, he roared.

"And what for?" said he. "Is *that* why I found you the other day hopping on one foot and swinging your arms like a distracted windmill? At your age, Nell!"

"Tim, I know the exercises look queer, but they give you great grace, the teacher says, and they make you very much less fleshy—stout—"

"Old lady," said Timothy Craven, "you're quite graceful enough for me, and I love every pound of you. Don't you let the girls bully you into frills!" And even when he lay dying, Craven said to her, faintly, "Nell, I've left you everything; I know you will do the best you can for the children, start the boys in business, and marry the girls off if they see the right kind of fellow; but—don't you let them bully you!"

Timothy had been a kind friend to Jerusha Arnold, always warm in her praise ever since the bad diphtheria time, when the two boys and Gertie fell ill and Tim nearly died. Not a nurse could be had for love or money; and Jerry had watched night and day. As for Jerry, she loved all her friends' children; but her soul clave to Gertie. Had she not come before the doctor and before the nurse, when Gertie was born? And had she not held Gertie on her shoulder the dreadful night through, when they thought Tim was dying, and the mother was with him? Her little fortune, after bequests in charity, was left to Gertrude Jerusha Arnold Craven, "in remembrance of many kindnesses showed to her old friend." So her will ran; and she often took it out and read it with satisfaction. But since Gertie went to the boarding school in Boston, and since the Craven boys had so increased the Craven fortune, although the boys were just the same, and called her "Cousin Jerry" and sent her costly Christmas gifts, the girls, she fancied, were changed.

A chill that could not be analyzed, but could be felt, was in the air. How should Gertie know the way in which the heart of a childless woman yearned over her? She could not see, in the old cabinet, the bundle of papers stored away with her mother's and the dead soldier's; and once when she did catch a glimpse of them by chance, how was she to guess that they were her own childish letters, written when they were away summers, to her "deer Cousin Jery," and the later and rarer letters of her youth.

"I guess it's natural," said the desolate woman. "Children don't notice that you're queer and old and poor; they only notice you love 'em; but when they grow up they *know*. I dont want to shame her before her beau. Yes, I expect it's natural; but, oh, Lord, it *hurts!*"

Yet it was not with Gertie's consent, that the slight had been given; and she drove away from Jerry's door with a clouded face. Ellen saw things differently. "I do hope that Miss Jerry won't be persuading mamma to invite her to the reception," she began.

Gertie, a pretty girl, who looked more like her dark-eyed, thin father than her fair, mild mother, turned her brilliant eyes for a moment on Ellen's frown.

"Cousin Jerry is not likely to persuade mamma or any one else to invite her to anything!" she said, coldly.

"Oh, you know what I mean. She'll seem cut up, and mamma will cry and beg her to come. 'I don't know what on earth I shall say to Jerry,' says mamma, the dear, soft-hearted thing. I told her to say nothing about the party at all. If she speaks she's lost. *I* didn't want her to get the things at Brandt's. We could have sent to Chicago perfectly well; then she wouldn't have heard it until it was all over with. It was your fault, Gertrude—you *would* go there!"

"I think we mortified poor Cousin Jerry enough without taking our trade away from the Brandt's," said Gertie. "I wish we hadn't given in to Hazel. Ellen, it strikes me we were snobs."

"Perhaps you think Hazel is a snob, too?"

"No," said Gertie, slowly, "I think Hazel

A COLONIAL DAME

is a fine young creature, but she is narrow, awfully narrow. It isn't Hazel I am angry at, it's myself. I'm *furious* at myself! I know my mother is worth a hundred of the fine people I met East, yet I find myself growing hot when I hear her talking about being 'plenty warm', and when she insists on pressing everything twice on the guests at a dinner, and—oh, you know. You," cried Gertie, in a burst of scorn, "are no better than I, and you didn't even stand up for poor, kind Cousin Jerry in the half-hearted way I did; but I declare I—I shall carry Reggy to see her!"

Ellen laughed, albeit with a rather shame-faced air.

"No, you won't," said she, "you daren't! And I daren't have her at the party. You are afraid of Reginald, and I am afraid of Mrs. Allen Masters."

Gertie did not answer for a while; she was redder than before, and seemed absorbed in thought. The landau bowled smoothly along the brick paving, past the new, tall shops and the rounded windows of the better streets which they were entering. Suddenly

A COLONIAL DAME

Gertie opened her lips to speak. What she would have said was: "Once Cousin Jerry gave me a ridiculously expensive present, that doll, when I was ten; and I overheard mamma say, 'Why, Jerry, how could you!' and she answered, 'Don't scold me, Ellie; you and the children are all I have!' If we are all she has, and we cast her off as not fine enough for our friends, how will she feel?" But this was never said, because at this instant Ellen spoke, pursuing her own train of thought. "Mrs. Masters met me on the street this morning, and asked me if our papers for the Colonial Dames were ready yet; she said she had sent hers and six other papers, and she wanted ours, because the applications were coming so fast, and she wanted us to be among the charter members."

"She's an old cat!" said Gertie.

"I believe she is," sighed Ellen; "and I believe you were right, and she only asked us to join the Colonial Dames because she thought we couldn't get in, and after we had committed ourselves and everybody knew—for she had spread it far and wide we were

A COLONIAL DAME

trying to join—it would be humiliating to fail."

"You can trust *her* for spreading it farther and wider," said Gertie, "that the poor Cravens feel so cut up; they wanted to join the Colonial Dames, and they couldn't find an ancestor. What did you say?"

"I said you were looking up the genealogical tree, and you would tell her."

"Much I've found," said Gertie, gloomily; "two solid nightmare weeks have I spent rummaging the New England genealogical register, until I dream of 'Early Marriages and Deaths in Sudbury,' and 'Genealogical Gleanings in old Braintree,' and inscriptions on porch doors; and for two months I have been writing people; and the only public thing that I can find any of our ancestors ever did was to hang a witch, and bring in a bill for five shillings for doing it—and that isn't gratifying to the family pride—"

"If he'd only been hanged for witchcraft himself?" suggested Ellen.

"But he wasn't; he hanged the other. There was a certain Gregory Craven who looked promising, but when I found a deed of his with 'Gregory Craven, His Mark,' I felt tolerably sure that he couldn't have been a governor, or assistant governor, or member of the colonial legislature for more than three years, or a secretary of state, or have written an election sermon, or been *any* eligible thing. So I gave him up. And the other Cravens, if they did anything, didn't belong to us—they were collaterals instead of directs—and if they belong to us, they didn't do anything public, except that one of Grandmamma Craven's ancestresses received relief from the selectmen as 'a poor, distressed widow woman subject to fits'—that's not gratifying, either!"

"It's awful!" moaned Ellen. "I wish you hadn't told me. What shall we do?"

"What we ought to do, if we weren't cowardly snobs, is to tell Mrs. Masters that we find our ancestors did not do anything of note, and say, 'Therefore, I pray thee, have me excused!'"

"But think of her triumph!"

"Think of the triumph of our consciences —but don't be scared, Ellen; I am a cowardly snob, too; I shall try to invent some plausible lie."

"We might—but mamma's ancestors are hopeless."

"Absolutely hopeless," agreed Gertie; "it would be a waste of time to look. Maybe some way out will suggest itself—some lie that is not too transparent." Ellen sighed, and they drove home in silence.

That night Gertie wrote to Reginald. She wrote with a frown and set teeth at the very end of her letter. "There is one dear friend of our family that I want you to meet. I hope you will like her. She is very plain, and not at all a fine lady" (she had lifted her pen to make the word gentlewoman, but threw it down, crying, "No, I won't deny poor Cousin Jerry *that*"), "but she has a heart of gold."

Reginald came a day earlier than she had expected him. He was a tall young fellow with a kind, ugly face and a simple manner. He blushed when he met Mrs. Craven, and said, "You're awfully good to let me have Gertie." He was interested in the town and in the people. He spoke with an English accent; but even Tim, who viewed him with an elder brother's critical eyes, could find no nonsense about him. In the afternoon, he walked with Gertie, affecting to look at the streets, really busy with a slim and dainty shape at his side. "I have seen Timothy," said he, "and Johnny's an old friend, and Hazel is a cousin—I've seen all your people, Gertie, except your Cousin Jerry. Take me to see her, can't you?"

A wicked cowardice whispered in Gertie's ear, "It is perfectly safe, she will be out; and you can please her by leaving cards." She listened, and afterward she believed she would have yielded; but even as she lifted her head to assent, a glittering phaeton wheeled by, turned; out between the lamps bent a delicate profile, and Mrs. Allen Masters' silvery voice called, "Oh, Miss Gertrude!"

The etiquette of a western town demanded that Reginald be presented. Mrs. Masters gave him one of her sweetest smiles.

"And—oh, Miss Gertrude, may we hope to have your papers to-morrow?" said she;

A COLONIAL DAME

"never mind the supplementals *one* ancestor is enough!"

"If you can catch him!" Gertie groaned, within. But she answered, "I will send you the papers or write to-morrow, Mrs. Masters."

"Thank you so much." And Mrs. Masters, smiling, passed on.

"What a ripping fine woman!" said Reggy.

A kind of disgust of herself, of her deference to the woman who had gone, of pretence of every kind swept over Gertie.

"Yes, she's handsome," she replied. "Reggy, you were speaking of Cousin Jerry; I don't think we should find her in; she goes out dressmaking by the day, and she would be gone. After dinner we might go."

She hurried her words a little, and her cheek wore a fine rose; but Reggy answered, easily, "Why, of course; I might have thought of that. Your mother told me about her. Don't you think there's something very touching in a friendship like theirs?"

"Yes," said Gertie. "Cousin Jerry is

worth a dozen ordinary women. You know we wanted her to live with us, but she was too independent."

"She's a fine old gentlewoman," declared Reggy, "and we will surely go to see her after dinner.

Gertie looked at him dubiously; her heart, which had lightened marvelously, sank again. What was Reggy's idea of a gentlewoman? Nevertheless, she took him to see Miss Jerry after dinner. The bakery doors were protected by screens, but the flies watched their chance, and were so many inside that they buzzed unpleasantly. The baker, in his shirt-sleeves, was wrapping up his wares for a crowd of barefooted children, some of whose faces needed washing. On the steps outside, the baker's wife rocked the baby.

"This is the place," said Gertie. She felt an instinct of defiance, of kinship, of fierce young protection, rising to battle with her own perception of the way Reggy must be viewing the home of Cousin Jerry. Reggy, however, at this moment was innocently greeting Mrs. Timothy Craven. She had just come out of the bakery—a slender young girl with regular features and a near-sighted frown.

"Gertie, *have* you tasted the cream cakes here?" she exclaimed, most amiably; "they're delicious. Filled with real cream!"

"They are nice," returned Gertie, calmly; "but we came to pay a visit to Cousin Jerry."

She was reminded of the experience (which she had once read) of a woman obliged to kill a chicken, who said that she trembled all the way to the fatal block, and could hardly see the hatchet, but the moment she lifted it her nerve returned, and she needed only to strike one blow.

"Didn't you know she lived here?" she continued, with a composure that struck herself as stony. "Come up-stairs and see her."

Even as Mrs. Tim hesitated, the bakery screens opened and Miss Jerry appeared, breathless. She had run all the way down-stairs to get a view of Reggy. She did not mean to let them see her, but when she heard Gertie's words her heart overcame her.

"Do come up," she urged, "and have some cream cakes and ice-cream up-stairs."

A COLONIAL DAME

Mrs. Tim was haughty, but she was well bred. She saw no civil way out of the snare, and meekly followed in Miss Jerry's wake. Up-stairs, in the little parlor, she politely tried to make conversation, and admired the cabinet.

"It's like one an old uncle of mine had," said she; "they are immensely interesting, these old rosewood things; yes, here's the secret drawer, you press the spring—oh, I beg your pardon!"

"It's nothing, said Miss Jerry, but she grew very pale; "just my little store of letters—thank you, Miss Gertie."

Gertie was as red as the other was pale. In replacing the letters she had caught her own name at the end of the childish scrawls, and seen her own photographs in a bundle; from the baby's card, faded and dull, to her latest carbon type, in a Paris gown.

"Do you like that gown?" said she, her eyes flashing. "I've another Paris gown to wear at the party. Cousin Jerry, what are *you* going to wear?"

Miss Jerry looked very strange. "I don't expect to go," said she, in a low tone.

A COLONIAL DAME

"But you *must*," said Gertie; "you must give up the whole day to it, and come early to arrange the flowers."

"I will fix the flowers, and gladly, Gertie, but I can't come."

"We'll see about that later," said Gertie, imperiously; "here's the ice-cream."

There was a little bustle of hospitality, and Gertie bent her hot cheeks over the white mound, while Mrs. Tim's lips stiffened; but she was too well bred to betray resentment before a stranger; as she phrased it, a stranger not of her own class; and she ate her ice-cream leisurely. Reggy, conscious of an awkward pause, essayed a new subject.

"I see, Hazel, you have started the Colonial Dames here," said he. "A lady spoke to Gertie about it on the street."

"Are you going to join, Miss Gertie?" said Miss Jerry.

"I'm afraid it isn't a question of wanting; we haven't the wherewithal of ancestors, Cousin Jerry," said Gertie, trying to laugh.

"You have at least five that *I* know of,"

A COLONIAL DAME

said Miss Jerry, and a streak of red crept up her cheek, "in your mother's family."

"Has your mother any colonial ancestors?" asked Mrs. Tim. She habitually called her mother-in-law "your mother," one of her little ways that irritated Gertie.

"She can get in on old Governor Winthrop, I expect," said Miss Jerry.

"You have the line proved?" Mrs. Tim could not help the ring of doubt in her voice.

Miss Jerry smiled rather grimly. She arose, and from the secret drawer she took out a long, white box, from which she removed and unfolded a roll of parchment decked with softly engraved medallions of coats of arms and a huge red seal, from which depended a blue and buff ribbon. Her finger traveled to the boldly written names and the engraved inscription, "*Miss Jerusha Winthrop Arnold has been duly elected a member of the Massachusetts society of the Colonial Dames of America, in the right of her ancestor, Governor John Winthrop.*"

"You can copy your paper and the dates and things from mine down to your great-grandmother, and your mother has got the certificates and family Bibles after that," said Miss Jerry.

"Your name is Winthrop," cried Gertie, "but I never thought—"

"Me neither," said Miss Jerry. "I didn't rightly know about it till last summer, on that trip your mother made me take. I met Cousin Phebe Abbot, and she's ancestor mad; and she got it all ready. I thought it might please you girls. I didn't get the certificate until last week, and, of course, I didn't want to speak before. I didn't even tell your ma. You'll have *her* join, of course!"

"Reginald is descended from the Winthrops," said Mrs. Tim.

"Then you are my Cousin Jerry, too, Miss Arnold," said Reggy, who looked very amused. He told Gertie afterward that he wouldn't have missed the scene for the world, that Hazel's face was a sight to behold.

Gertie did not notice his amusement; afterward she laughed; but it was another emotion she felt at the time, which made her fling her arms about Miss Jerry, between laughing and crying, and exclaim: "You gave me the prettiest doll I ever had, Cousin Jerry, and now you give me the prettiest badge!"

Mrs. Tim arose. She said she must go; but she smiled on Miss Jerry, and asked her to come to see her Copley miniatures.

"And you will come to the party," cried Gertie, "and wear your badge, and be the first Colonial Dame here!"

"Yes, do come," said Mrs. Tim.

And Reggy coughed and looked out of the window before he added his entreaties.

Miss Jerry did come. She wore a new gown presented by Gertie, which was vastly admired by the whole building. Everybody assisted at the toilet, and she departed in the presence of the entire body of tenants, who almost cheered her. Reggy was very attentive to her, and called her "Cousin Jerry." Many people told the Cravens that Miss Arnold was a distinguished-looking woman. The same people said that she had a sweet, quaint way of talking.

"She is an old-fashioned New England gentlewoman," said Mrs. Tim. "I like the way they talk."

A COLONIAL DAME

And Reggy ducked his head and actually winked at Gertie.

As for Ellen, she was busy crushing Mrs. Masters. She brought her up, and presented her in form to "My Cousin, Miss Arnold."

"Miss Arnold will explain our line of descent," said she, grandly; "please tell her, Cousin Jerry. The Winthrop one, I mean."

"Cousin Jerry" the Colonial Dame has remained ever since to all the Craven family, including Mrs. Tim; while Mrs. Craven, a Dame now herself, is treated with so much consideration that she feels the liveliest gratitude to Miss Jerry, old Governor Winthrop of illustrious memory, and the Colonial Dames of America.

A Jealous Woman

"NOW put the basket on the lounge and move the lounge to the window."

"I'm 'fraid it hurt Mrs. Rogers—after such a bad night."

"Never mind. Move it!"

Hulda had only been a month with the Rogerses, but she knew enough not to disregard that particular intonation. Being a Swede and not a Frenchwoman, she did not shrug her plump shoulders; but she shot an eyeblink through the crack in the door, at a woman in the hall, before she wheeled the lounge as directed. Drops beaded the brow of the woman on the lounge; she grew paler and frowned with pain, yet not a sigh escaped her lips.

The Swede eyed her covertly, admiration and disapproval both in her heavy, fair face. "Mrs. Rogers want anyt'ing else?"

"No, thank you. I've got the undershirts to mend? Yes. Well, you dust the sitting-room with a damp cloth—it's not dusting, it's only swapping dust, to dust with a feather duster. And tell Susan to have marrowfat peas instead of the string-beans for dinner. Mr. Rogers doesn't like beans; and you can help Susan iron so she can make some ice-cream. Some bread and butter and tea is all I shall want. You needn't toast the bread."

"Won't I stay wid Mrs. Rogers? Won't s'e want some—"

"Nothing. You go and help Susan. I have a bell if I need you."

Hulda went, nothing loth, to join Susan Pierce at the foot of the stairs. Susan was a little, gaunt, plain woman in a scant-skirted blue calico, such as the Amana colonists wear. Indeed, before she married a worldly farmer and became his widow, Susan was of the colony herself—it is only an hour's ride by steam, from the little University town; and she always kept a hint of it in her austere garb for work or leisure.

"Well?" said Susan Pierce.

"S'e looks awful sick, but s'e says s'e don't want me. S'e made me move the lounge so s'e can watch him from window. S'e say you make ice-cream and I help you, and s'e only like bread and butter—not toast bread—"

" 'Cause it's ironing day," interrupted Susan. "Some ways she's real considerate; and I never did see sech a housekeeper as her, sick or well."

"Nor I never see such a *beautiful* kitchen, such pretty white sink and lots of t'ings to cook out. And no company—"

"I wisht there was more company. No childern and no company makes a house dull. But we don't lack for good eating when *he's* home. I never seen a man so pampered. I guess his second won't give him a clean shirt every day. Well, you going to help with the ironing?"

Hulda was going to help. She much preferred a gossip over the ironing-board to a silent morning with the invalid. Smilingly she led the way to the laundry and began at a great, damp bundle. The wide west door of the laundry was open, as were the two south windows—windows and doors being covered with wire, against which the lavish morning-glory vines were tapping softly gorgeous bells of purple and red, not yet shrunken by the sun. Morning or afternoon it was always shady under the laundry windows, because of the great cherry tree which glittered now with little dots of flame. The birds were singing, and a bluejay scolded a sparrow with grotesque travesty of wrath. Through the greenery was a vista of pastures where cattle were grazing among the trees, a swell of shorn hay-field which glistened like yellow-white silk, another field where the reaper was moving; and beyond, the lovely, rich green undulations of a field of corn, that dipped into a snowy, shifting mountain range of clouds. Once, when Professor Rogers, as he was always called (although really he had never advanced beyond the modest state of "instructor") was teaching English literature in the State University, he asked an Iowa boy, what, in his judgment, was the most beautiful object in nature, to which the answer came promptly:

"A field of corn just ready to tassel—when the lines are drawn straight!"

In the dry years that had quenched all his young ambitions, often, Ben Rogers had looked on "the big corn-field," recalling the lad's words, and always with an obscure moving of the heart. Even Susan Pierce, who did not incline to sentiment, drew a pleased sigh, as she gazed, that morning. "Corn's looking real well," said Susan.

"It's a nice farm," agreed Hulda. "Ain' it queer when folks own such a nice farm and have such a pretty house dey don't be happy? Just 'cause s'e's so yealous; but I don't see but what e's a nice mans."

"And he *is* a nice man, Hulda Oleson," cried Susan; "prompt to his meals and ready to praise 'em, and grateful when you do things, and always wipes his feet in muddy weather. *I* call the professor 'bout as good as they make 'em. But I ain't denying she's jealous; she always was."

"W'at of?"

"Everybody. That's the mischief of it. 'Tain't only the women. They're the worst, of course; but she's jealous of his friends.

A JEALOUS WOMAN

Why, she was so jealous of an old dog he had that he thought the world on, she wouldn't let him have the critter in the house, not even on the *pia*zza. Many's the time I've seen him a-setting on the grass so's to have Jumbo near him. He was a little raggedy dog, but he called him Jumbo 'cause he had such a spirit. The professor, he used to wash that dog and comb him and teach him tricks; and then, when he got him learned, one day he tied a blue ribbon to his collar and combed him nice and sen him in—on the *pia*zza—to show off his tricks to Mrs. Rogers. I was peeking 'round the door, for I knowed what the professor was up to; and he had the dog go through all his little tricks—they was real cute—and some way the critter had a real anxious look in his eye, like he knew he was trying to please. But when he was through, and the professor, who looked 'most 's anxious as the doggie, turns to her and says, 'I'm going to give this accomplished little animal to you, my dear, if you will accept him,' she said she didn't want him. The professor looked at her one minute, never said a word, jest looked. Then he picked up the dog, and looked at him real affectionate like. 'I'm sorry,' says he; 'I thought he'd be company to you when I was away in the fields. You'd have grown fond of him, maybe.' He walked off a few steps and he stopped, maybe hoping she'd call him back; but she didn't. She sat there looking mad —awful mad; and he took the dog off. He patted it as he was walking off. Next morning that dog was dead—poisoned!"

"I *hela verlden!*" cried Hulda. "Say, did s'e poison him?"

Mrs. Pierce bore harder on the flatiron than seemed necessary. "I ain't saying. All I know is, there he was; and the professor found him all limp, lying on the *pi*azza step, like he'd tried to get to his master. He felt *bad*. I guess they had a quarrel. Fact is, I did hear him say (as I passed the door): 'You might have left me a dog!' "

"What did he want to give it to her if s'e was such cruel vomans?"

"She wouldn't have been cruel to it if she'd a-taken it. No, I guess he knowed how she felt, and that was how he tried to

A JEALOUS WOMAN

save the critter. But, land! that's only one thing. I've seen her when he was in the university and they lived down-town—I've seen her refuse to set down at table when he brought a friend to dinner—right before the man, too. Of course nobody was going to call on him or take a meal with him if they was exposed to sech treatment. And the girls in his classes—oh my! She went to one of them and told her, 'You let my husband alone!' The girl was a real nice girl and hadn't done a thing 'cept let him walk home with her one day when it rained and she hadn't no umbrella. She was mad enough. Then Mis' Rogers took to going to all his classes, herself. I guess 'twas that shamed him so he gave up his job. Maybe he had to, for there was an awful sight of talk, her acting that way. That's how he come to buy this farm. Ruther, *she* bought it. She's got the money. I will say for her she knows how to run a farm—her folks was farmers, you know. It's her more'n him made the money. They've been more peacefuller sence she come out here. He's dretful careful for one thing. But when he got kinder

A JEALOUS WOMAN

interestid in politics and they was talking of running him for the legislatoor, she put a stop to that in a jiffy. I've often wondered she bought here, next to the Morrills, them jest across the road. Maybe she didn't know 'bout how he was supposed to have been engaged to Hetty Morrill; or maybe— for she's awful sharp in a bargain—her gittin' this place so cheap on a mortgage, was what moved her. Anyhow she done it—she herself. And for the better part of fifteen year she's been jealous of poor Miss Morrill."

"Say, how'd he come to marry her? Why didn't he marry Miss Morrill? s'e seem such nice lady."

"So she is, too; took care of her pa for seventeen years, most, him helpless and she running the place and making a good living with early vegetables, and not only not calling on the boys who are all married and got families, but helping dress and educate their children. And she, not letting the professor much's cross the threshold nor let 'em have milk when one of their cows died sudden and t'other one was dry! He never did step his foot over the doorsill till old Dr. Morrill died sudden in the night, and he would go over next morning to help. Why, Hulda Oleson, she had the gall to be worked up over *that!* Had hysterics and threatened to kill him. She hollered and screamed so you could hear her in the kitchen; wanted him to promise he'd not go to the funeral. But I'm thankful to say he did go; but he ketched it, afterwards, I guess."

She paused to adjust the shining folds of damask that she was ironing, and her thoughts took a new turn. "Ain't that pretty table linen?" she sighed; "there ain't a lady on the faculty—not even the president's wife's got finer table-cloths and napkins than she has; and she's been ailing ten years, and only able to ride round in a wheeled chair. But twict a year she'd be lifted into the phaeton and druv to the depot with the chair in the wagon follerin' after, and she'd go to Chicago and buy things and, as she says, see the fashions and give him a real good time. She went when it was jest torture to her and she wa'n't nowise able. Never mind, she was going; and she'd go

A JEALOUS WOMAN

with him to the theaters, too. But the last year she ain't able to leave her lounge; but you notice she won't move down-stairs—that's so she kin look over the fields from one winder and over the Morrills' from the other and watch him good. She's at the Morrill winder (I call it), this mornin'."

"I t'ink e'd git wore out."

"I guess he does. I come to 'em when they was first married. And then I got married and lived on my own farm till Pierce died, and then she wanted me back and I was lonesome after my girl married and I hadn't earned enough to live like I wanted, so I come; and I can tell you, I seen a change. When I was first here, they'd have hot quarrels; but then she'd come round and cry and beg him to forgive her and they'd make up and seem real loving to each other. Now, they don't seem to have so much fights, he's looking old and discouraged and broke, and he's patient with what would 'a' sent him a-swearing, once. But they don't have none of them old making-up times, either. I never seen him real mad at her but that one time 'bout the dog and one time when she shot Miss Hetty's bronze turkey. It someway got into our yard and she was in her wheel-chair and she got her pistil fetched her and plugged it full—a-settin' right on the grass and Miss Hetty running to save it. That's the only time *she* ever come in our gate! Professor wanted to give her another, but she wouldn't take it."

"Ain t it awful old folkses like im and er going on dat way!" cried Hulda, to whom, as to many young people, love, except in its most decorous and placid forms, appeared the property of youth alone. "W'y! e must be fifty years ole—and s'e's ol'er!" she exclaimed, in a tone almost of awe at the shameful spectacle.

"Fifty ain't so *awful* old," returned Mrs. Pierce, drily, " 'specially for a man. Tho' he is a good deal dried up and runted by what he's gone through and being out in the sun. She's some older'n him, I dunno how much. I know when he married her, he was twenty-eight—"

" 'Ow'd e come to marry er?"

"I dunno ezactly. He was teaching, and the girls were all going on 'bout him. She

A JEALOUS WOMAN

was a only child, and her folks left her money, and she took it into her head she wanted to be a trained nurse, and she come here to be in the hospital. And he was took sick with typhoid fever and, fact is, she saved his life with her nussing; and when he got well he married her. *I* always thought he was in love with Hetty Morrill and her with him; but they had a fool quarrel, and then he couldn't make it up 'cause he went off and married this one. Well, I will say when she ain't jealous, she's good as gold to him. And I can't help being kinder sorry for her lately, sence that young flyaway niece of Miss Morrill's come to 'tend the university and stay at her aunt's. Minnit I set my eyes on her I knowed she'd make trouble. She'd a young feller with her; but she's one of the flirty kind, and she druv up to our gate and begun making eyes at the professor right before her! Well, she's kept it up. I dunno whether she's mean or just mis*chie*vous! But I'd think a lot more of her if she helped her aunt more 'bout the house.''

Susan folded the table-cloth before she

A JEALOUS WOMAN

spoke again, this time with a lower voice: "Say, Hulda, don't she strike you as sicker all the time? She never complains, but she's give up doing things. I guess he won't have to wait long to be quit of her jealous ways. And yet, I will say when she ain't jealous, she's awful kind and good. I ain't nothing to complain of myself, neither."

While the women talked Elsie Rogers was lying on her lounge by the window. She had been a pretty girl, with a plump, dashing, high-colored comeliness. Now, she was thin and sallow. Her skin showed the sickly pallor of old ivory There were fretful wrinkles about the lips that had been like rose-leaves when young Ben Rogers used to lecture on English literature and quote Swinburne in his beautiful voice.

She could hear the very cadence of his voice, again, telling how the gods made man of "fire and the falling of tears and a handful of shifting sand."

> "He weaves and is clothed with derision,
>   He sows and he shall not weep,
> His life is a watch or a vision
>   Between a sleep and a sleep."

A JEALOUS WOMAN

A spark glowed in Elsie Rogers's smoldering black eyes, as her thoughts went back to those days.

"That's true enough," she muttered, "and I am clothed with derision, I've given him *everything*. He was poor; he owed money when I married him. I paid it all off for him. And when I came into my money I bought this farm for him and ran it. Much *he* knew of farming! And I've stood between him and everything. And it's been like hell, all the time. And now when I know I've got to die, I keep thinking of him, instead—what's that?"

She raised herself painfully on her elbow. She could see the Morrill doorway brightened by a dainty shape in pink dimity, a golden-brown head, with a broad leghorn hat crowned with roses and decked in long pink ribbon streamers that flew loose in the breeze.

A little hiss of pain parted Elsie Rogers's lips when she twisted her shoulders to watch the pink figure trip down the yellow streak of road. It stopped, a little space further on; and the roses fluttered gayly, while

A JEALOUS WOMAN

the girl leaned on the fence and talked with a little man in blue overalls. Elsie could almost hear the laughter. The talk was brief, and directly the girl in pink was tripping back to the house, while Ben (for the man was her husband) turned on his heel and came frowning towards her. But he did not mount the stairs. Ten minutes, perhaps, passed, during which she heard his footsteps below, the footsteps of a person moving about a room, not passing from one room to another, and then she saw him come out, having changed his rough garb for a white crash suit and his new straw hat.

"That's why he has got to keeping his clothes down-stairs, is it?" muttered his wife. She smiled bitterly as the colt and the new buggy with the red wheels were brought out to the gate; more bitterly as Ben drove the new buggy up to the shabby brown gate of the Morrills. It was no surprise to her that the dainty pink skirts should flutter again through the doorway and flutter into the buggy, while Ben stood by the horse's head. It was no surprise to have Sadie Morrill fling the insolent challenge of her smile up at the invalid's window, as the dust volleyed under the red wheels.

For a second the jealous wife burrowed her head in the pillow with a sick moan; but she lifted it at the creak of the Morrills' door. Hester Morrill, it was now, who stood in the doorway and the sunshine, a slender woman with gray in her brown hair and lines about the patient brown eyes.

"My! doesn't she look old in that blaze!" the watcher gloated, venomously; "she's watching him, too. Does it hurt, Miss? I hope it does. I'm not the only one to have my heart cut out. How do you like it, now it's your turn? Wearing baby-blue calico, because it used to be becoming! And you can see the gray in her hair across the street. But she curls it on papers every morning, just the same. Trying to look young! You fool! can't you see he hasn't eyes for you any more? Oh, I've seen the look in his eyes many a night when he'd be sitting out on the piazza with me, his wife, but looking over to your old house—that you don't paint once in five years—hoping to catch a glimpse of you; and because you never spoke to each other, do you suppose I didn't know what he was thinking of and didn't hate you? I did; but I don't now. I've been jealous of you for twenty years; but I'm not jealous of you now. Do you hear, Hester Morrill? I'm not jealous of you, now!" She barked the sentence aloud, in a spasm of passion, forgetting the open window. Was it possible that the other woman heard? She lifted her eyes. They shone, gentle, sad and quiet; and there was in them, as they fell full on Elsie, something sorrowful but not angry. For the first time in her life Elsie felt that Hester pitied her. It was a queer, heavy emotion that made her involuntarily lower her own gaze. When, with an instant reaction of defiance, she looked up again Hester was gone; and, what was most queer, the doorway looked empty and lonesome. Then she was conscious that Hester, after fifteen years of silence, had nodded and smiled. "I almost wish I'd beckoned to her," she thought, half dazed by her own mood, "I believe she would have come over. It would have been fun to see her wince when I talked about how pretty Sadie is." She caught her breath softly, and her head rolled as she used to roll it in unbearable pain (at night when she would not moan for fear of waking Ben), while she whispered: "I'd love to kill that Sadie!"

A spasm of pain seized her even in the words, and for a few moments her physical torment was too acute to let her mind get away from it; but at last the breath came painfully back to her body, the overtaxed heart beat more quietly, and she took up her needlework. "I'm only killing myself the quicker," she said; "and I would like to get Ben's underclothes mended up and everything ready for him for winter, if I could, *first*. She's a careless, bold-faced jig that's let her aunt mend her stockings while she flirts with the boys. And Ben's never had to ask for a button."

An hour went by—two hours. She sat, propped on her pillows, sewing most of the time, but, occasionally, from sheer weakness, the needle would slip out of her limp fingers. At times, also, she flung the work aside with a groan and wrung her hands and swayed her body, like one in a torment. A score of vivid emotions wrenched her features; alike only in the misery that was in all of them. Sometimes it was wild to frenzy, and she had the face of a cruel maniac; sometimes it was more remorseful than angry and the tears ran down her thin cheeks.

She was in this softer, kinder frame, when the rattle of wheels penetrated the room. "I won't look out," she thought; "I wont spy on him."

The wheels stopped. She craned her neck and pressed her face against the wire screen. She could see the streak of yellow roadway drawn straight through the green corn-fields. She could see the modest brown house of the Morrills, a rectangle and an ell with a narrow piazza in the angle. But there was no buggy in sight. "He has stopped at the lower gate," she reflected bitterly; and, not for the first time, she called him a coward.

"But I won't say a mean word to him this time," she added. "I'm too sick to quarrel with him. I will be good."

A JEALOUS WOMAN

The buggy-wheels rattled again. The horse came in sight, then the buggy, in which sat her husband alone. He looked up at the window and lifted his hat.

She did not return the salute; he saw only the averted oval of his wife's cheek; *she* saw Sadie Morrill's pink skirt behind the flower beds. She could not smile on her husband, but she gnawed her under-lip. "No, I won't say a word!" she resolved.

She could hear his step on the stair. It was the heavy, springless step of a tired, elderly man. He entered the chamber with a diffident air. "Well, I've been to town," said he.

"So I see; you and Sadie Morrill; I saw you driving off together," answered Elsie. She had meant to control herself; but at this moment, happening to look across the street, she saw Sadie come blithely out and sink luxuriously in the hammock, where she began to swing and read and eat candy out of a pink box; and an access of rage drove the words out of Elsie's heart and fired the tone.

The man sat down on the edge of the

A JEALOUS WOMAN

nearest chair; he was, no doubt, as desperately uncomfortable as he looked. He was a small man. He had not grown stout with years, but rather had withered. When he was twenty-eight, the handsome young scholar whose face haunted the girls' dreams, he wore a mustache with curly ends. Now, at fifty, he still wore a mustache with curly ends, although his shaven cheeks were wrinkled and hollow and the mustache gray. Ben Rogers looked older than his years or his farmer's life demanded; he looked crushed and tired. His eyes, which had been full of fire, were dull.

"Yes, their horse is lame; they've only got one, now," he answered without resentment, fingering his hat and talking into it. "It seemed unneighborly to let her walk in the heat. I was going to town, anyhow."

"Did you have to carry her back, too?"

"I suppose the walk back is just as sunny."

Elsie Rogers laughed spitefully. "Did you have to give her candy because it was sunny?" He shot a glance over to the piazza, and his tanned cheek flushed. "Or perhaps *you* didn't give her the candy; she has lots of other beaux, you know."

"She may have the entire university for anything *I* care, undergraduates, laws and medics—and dentals thrown in!" cried Rogers.

"*Did* you give her the candy?"

"Well, if I did; now, Elsie—"

He was arrested by the change in her face, it was so ghastly. He got on his feet to help her; but the attack, whatever its nature, which had squeezed the color out of her skin, passed as quickly as it came. The blue shadow faded away from her mouth; she even smiled. "Ben," said she, in a changed tone, "do you know I'm going to die?"

He came over to her before he answered, and took a chair by her side. His face was still flushed. "Don't talk that way, my dear," he said, awkwardly. "We—we'll change doctors if you say so."

"It's easier to change doctors than diseases, Ben. Oh, I know; and you know too. I don't need to ask you and have you try to lie to me. You knew before I did.

A JEALOUS WOMAN

You haven't been cross with me for a month. I saw you out walking in the pasture with Doctor a month ago Sunday; and when you came in you kissed me. You hadn't kissed me—first—for a long while. And that night you didn't sit out on the piazza and smoke. You came right up and fanned me. It was a hot night. I was so pleased. But I've thought it out, since. Ben, there's a lot to think of when one is going to die. I had the lawyer up and made my will. Do you know what I did?"

"I have never asked you about any of the wills you have made, Elsie," said he, with a show of pride, the first sign of emotion given by him.

"I left you everything—the farm, the bank-stock, the town lots, every cent I have in the world; it's more than sixty thousand, Ben; everything—so long's you remain a widower."

His hand did not quiver on her hair; in fact, he smiled a little.

"So I presumed, Elsie; that's very generous of you; but I hope you will be long spared to me."

A JEALOUS WOMAN

"You can go back to town and be a professor again and write like you used to want—"

"Ah, my dear," he interrupted, wincing; "no, that's over and gone. I can't pick up a profession. They wouldn't have me. I'm a back number. The young men would laugh at me. The world has been going on while I have rusted by the wayside. Besides, I like farming. I've done pretty well at it —with your money."

He took a light tone over it; nevertheless she could see that she was touching the quick. She flashed out: "You're a dozen times better than those young upstarts; you've sense, you've experience, you've—"

"I haven't technique. I don't know the new methods. Why, my dear, fancy yourself back in a hospital. You were a good nurse—no one knows that better than I; but where would you be in a modern hospital with the new antiseptic methods? It's the same with me. Do you understand?"

She understood, whether she would confess it or not; and he perceived as much.

"Perhaps it is just as well," he went on in his patient voice, dull like his eyes; "all my fine dreams might have come to nothing, and here I have at least made two blades of grass grow where only one blade would have grown. That's something."

"Confess," she cried, suddenly raising herself on one elbow and speaking shrilly, while her eyes burned—"confess, I've been a clog on you. I made you leave your profession, I wouldn't let you go into politics—"

"Thereby no doubt saving my money and my time, and probably my self-respect. Don't reproach yourself for that, Elsie; you've no need."

"I've estranged you from every old friend you had—"

'Now, Elsie, what is the use of going into that again? I'm not accusing you. You'll bring on an attack. There, there!" He tried clumsily to soothe her, and she burst into rasping laughter.

"Oh, how reasonable you are! how cool and calm and reasonable and forbearing! *Ben!*"

He jumped. "Yes? what's the matter?" He looked bewildered.

"Ben, I know I've been a clog on you. I know I've been jealous of you and made you ashamed and unhappy. Our life's been a hell; do you know why? It's *your* fault! Because you *never* loved me! If you *had* loved me and I had been sure of it, *once* sure of it, I'd have been able to control myself. But you never did love me—"

"Elsie," said her husband, with an effort at sternness, "I married you—"

"You married me because I asked you— oh, let me alone! I'm going to talk it out, this once more. You were sick and weak, and I'd saved your life, and you'd quarreled with your girl, and you took me to comfort you. And, at first, when I was young and pretty and a slave at your feet, if you'd only let other women alone, you had some kind of feeling for me; but it wasn't *love*. Not your *soul's* love, which I wanted. And I knew it, and I raged against it; and the more I gave way to the devil in me, the stronger he grew. Ben, he's too strong for me, now; he won't let me be kind and patient to you the little time I've got left to be with you. I want to be—O God! I *do* want to be! I want to leave some memories of me that will soften your heart to me; but

A JEALOUS WOMAN

I can't. It chokes me! I keep seeing you with other women, *young* women, pretty, laughing, happy, glad I'm out of the way! You're glad, too! No, you shan't touch me; you've killed me! The doctor said—excitement—"

"Elsie, do be sensible," begged the man.

"I wish I *hated* you!"

Ben only proffered a glass in which he had poured a few drops from a vial, and said as kindly as he could, that she must not excite herself, it would be bad.

She struck the glass from his hand and burst into screams and wild laughter. Down-stairs two women exchanged glances.

"It's kinder awful," said Hulda; "do you t'ink the pain is so dreadful?"

" 'Tain't pain," said Susan Pierce, "there wasn't made the pain could get a screech outer *her*. Now, she's stopped—*that's* the pain!"

She had stopped—suddenly, as Ben at his wits' end was about to leave the room and summon Susan; she ceased her clamor and gasped, "Oh, don't go, Ben. It's the pain again! Please do something!"

A JEALOUS WOMAN

He was quick to do something now. He held her in his arms, he administered the remedies with which all the household were grown familiar; and in the midst of it her marvelous patience, in so strange contrast with the crazy abandon of a moment previous, extorted his admiration. It was easy for him now to whisper tender words, for there was a moment when her soul seemed slipping away from him. His own was chilled by the thought, Had *he* brought on this attack? But it passed; she was able to smile wanly up in his face, and to lay a feeble hand on his cheek, murmuring: "Poor Ben! I'm so sorry I was bad to you."

There had always been a charm about her in her gentler moments; even now, faded and ill as she was, it asserted its power over him. Impulsively, after years of struggle, in a single moment of pity he gave up the contest. "Elsie," he said, "would you feel better if—if I promised you—what you have asked me?"

A light of rapture transfigured her face until it was young again. "Oh, Ben!" she breathed, faintly.

That was all; but it was enough. He kissed her. "I promise you, Elsie," said he.

Susan Pierce sat with the invalid that afternoon. Susan hemmed a blue apron. Her lips were compressed.

"How did Mr. Rogers like his peas?" was Mrs. Rogers's first question.

"He didn't tech 'em," replied Susan, crustily, "nor the ice-cream, neither. He said he guessed the heat made him sick, and he only drunk a cup of coffee—forgot the cream to that, too." She watched the cloud gather over Mrs. Rogers's face with a certain pity. "Can't help it," she thought, "that man's been made to do something he didn't want to, and I guess I know what; and he ain't got nobody to help him but me." Her sharp eyes had taken in the whole room, not missing a charred document in the grate. Elsie's glance ran after hers. "That's my will," she said, using the reckless frankness that was part of her untamed nature; "it wasn't just to Mr. Rogers's liking, so I burned it, this morning."

A JEALOUS WOMAN

Susan thought a nod quite enough for the demands of respectful sympathy.

Elsie lay back on her lounge, too weak to work. She idly watched the sunlight flickering through the maples in front of the Morrill yard and the flutter of the pink dimity skirts on the lawn. Sadie was playing croquet with a student who lived in town, hence had not flown with the rest, after commencement. Her laughter rippled above his deeper notes. He laughed a good deal.

Elsie watched them; and a wave of bitterness rose again in her soul. The promise which had so comforted her had made him wretched. He regretted that unfeeling girl. She turned to Susan, who sewed on with as little emotion as an Indian.

"Susan," said she, "did you ever know any men who promised their wives not to marry again?"

"Yes'm," said Susan.

"And did they keep their word?"

"Not them I knowed," said Susan, after a conscientious interval of meditation; "well, I only knowed three, but a neighbor of mine knowed two she used to tell me 'bout. They all married within the year. I dunno what excuses they give to their consciences, 'cept old Captain White; *he* told me, himself, he promised his wife 'cause she was awful sick, and says he, 'I told her that jest like I'd have told her any other lie, to make her easy!' I guess it's nature's to blame more'n the men."

Elsie made no comment. She asked no more questions; but she remembered the old man that she knew in her childhood, whose wife had extorted such a promise. *He* had been faithful to his word; but she thought of him with no lightening of the weight on her heart; for it was common talk that his wife's unmarked, neglected grave was the outward sign of his resentment. In truth, it was rumored that he had said, once, that he hated his wife. Would Ben come to hate her as well as those invisible fetters which she had bound on him?"

"Susan," said Elsie, "you go to town on the street cars and have Judge Black come back with you."

"Right now?" said Susan.

"Fast's you can."

A JEALOUS WOMAN

There was nothing left for Susan but to go, querying within herself whether she had not hurt rather than helped Ben Rogers's cause.

Elsie lay back on the lounge. She suffered, but the forces in her being were too low for any paroxysm. "I guess I'm beaten," she said, drearily. "Oh, if God would only let me stop loving Ben and die in peace!"

The laughter of the young people opposite came in more clearly. She hated their youth, their gayety, their rampant health. "I've got to die and leave him to that girl!" she thought; "he wont keep his word—and the will's burned!"

She saw Hester Morrill come to the window and drop the shade. A moment after Sadie and the young man came on to the porch. He was persuading her to go somewhere with him, to some merrymaking.

"I don't know what Aunt Hetty will say," said she; and he answered: "Oh, the old lady is all right!"

"The old lady!" Why yes, Hester was not young, in spite of her trim figure and her careful curls. She wondered if Hester had overheard. Then, she saw the fingers of a hand pull the curtain a little further, from within; and she knew that Hester had overheard. The young people were sitting in the hammock, eating candy out of the pink box. "I'm going in to ask Auntie to make some lemonade for us," exclaimed the girl. She went in and came back; and after a little while Miss Hester appeared and left them a salver with a generous jug of lemonade.

They sat on the piazza for more than an hour; and Elsie could see the aunt weeding in the garden. A strange feeling took possession of her. She sided with the elderly woman who had lost everything, against this brutal and greedy youth.

For an hour or more she lay, thinking deeply but quietly. Then the lawyer came.

Rogers heard of the lawyer's presence when he came. He was not frank like his wife; he merely sank his gaze to the ground and his lips twitched. Susan Pierce continued: "She passed a pretty good, quiet afternoon, I guess. 'Bout five she sent for me and had me take the biggest bronze

A JEALOUS WOMAN

turkey over to Miss Morrill's with her compliments."

Ben started violently. "Did—did Miss Morrill accept it?"

"Yes, sir; and she sent word could she come to see Mrs. Rogers, and Mrs. Rogers she sent word she'd be glad to see her."

Ben slowly let the breath that he had drawn into his lungs leave him, in a deep sigh. "Thank you, Susan," said he, and turned away.

He found his wife quiet and gentle; but plainly was not disposed to talk; nor did he disturb her.

In the morning Hester came. "And she came jest as ca'm and easy as if she'd been coming right along all these fifteen years. But I'd give a good deal," said Susan, "to hear what's going on behind that door, this minute!"

However, she could not hear; Hester Morrill never told any living creature. She sat down by the lounge wheeled to its old place. Elsie noticed that she wore a black gown and her hair was drawn smoothly back from her forehead.

A JEALOUS WOMAN

"Did you think it was queer I sent for you?" said Elsie.

"I don't think it was really queer," said Hester. "I was glad to come."

"I sent for you," Elsie continued in a low voice, "because I'm beaten. You know I've hated you—"

"Yes," said Hester; "but I know you don't hate me now."

"No. There's only one person I hate now. It isn't you. *You* are sorry for me."

"I am from my heart."

"Yet you loved Ben, and you know I've made him miserable. He has had no career, and but for me he might have been almost anything. He has had no friends, no ambition; I've ruined his life; you can't deny it."

"You never meant to hurt him," said Hester.

"No, you're right, I never did. One way no woman could have worked harder for him. But he said to me once, that a man wanted something more than money in the bank and a comfortable home and a good dinner. I didn't give it to him. I don't believe there

A JEALOUS WOMAN

was ever anybody so unhappy in this world as I've been. But the Bible's right, jealousy is crueler than the grave. No matter what I'd resolve, the moment I saw him caring for anything but me, I *had* to tear it away from him. Now, I am going to die, and I want to tear it away from him worse than ever. Hester Morrill, did he really love you?"

"I thought he did," said Hester. She did not flush, she who had guarded her secret for twenty years; it seemed to her that the absolute truthfulness of this doomed woman compelled an absolute truthfulness from her.

"I never thought he loved *me*," said Elsie. "Oh, I was young and pretty, and you know what men are; he had a feeling for me for a little while. But when that died out there was nothing left. He was sorry for me and he was afraid of me. That's all. And I loved him so I was willing to take loving words and caresses that I'd *begged* for. Hester, do you think, you that lost him but kept his—his respect, do you think you suffered like me that won him?"

A JEALOUS WOMAN

"No," said Hester. There were tears in her eyes.

"And now, I've got to die, and he won't have me to care for him. Hester, he isn't a man to take care of himself. He needs somebody. He'll lose money; he'll miss his comforts that he makes so light of because they have been as steady as the sun. Yet, knowing that, I've made him promise not to marry again. I've thought it out; I've thought of killing him—"

She hesitated and peered keenly at Hester.

"You poor soul," said Hester, "what good would that do? You can't kill his soul; and you'll have to meet him, you with that awful sin on you—"

"I'd be more afraid to meet him than I would to meet God," cried Elsie.

"I suppose so. You oughtn't to be; but you're a woman. I should be in your place."

"And I've thought of killing *her*."

A flush that burned for a moment on Hester's pale cheek and then ebbed away, told that she did not need a name. "What would be the good to stain your soul by making him care for her the more—if he does care for her."

"Then, Hester, what am I going to do?"

Hester bent her head; and Elsie, with a certain awe, was aware that she was praying. When she lifted her face it was no longer sad; but on it glowed a lofty flame which poor Elsie could not understand, but which instinctively she reverenced. She groped for Hester's hand and held it. "My dear," said Hester, "do you love Ben well enough to want him to be happy, even if you are not the one to give him happiness?"

Elsie shook her head. "No, I can't. I want to make him happy myself."

"But you want him to remember you with kindness, with regret. Nobody can watch over him the way you have. Why, I—" the flush came back a second—"I have been grateful to you when he was sick, seeing how you cared for him. Do you suppose he won't miss that care? Don't poison the sorrow he will feel by trying to chain him to your grave! Be good to him, be generous, win his gratitude and his respect—"

"Do you know," interrupted Elsie, "that

you are pleading against yourself for Sadie Morrill?"

"I am pleading for *his* future, for freedom to choose, which is more to any manly man than anything else. How do you know she will not make him happy? How do you know he will choose her? Let him be free."

"And give him the money, too?"

"He's worked for it as well as you."

Elsie's face remained hard.

"And could you endure to leave him, knowing he would be poor and have to begin life over at fifty, and maybe lack the luxuries you have made necessary to him, have to pinch and slave—"

"Stop!" Elsie cried; "you know I can't. You know I am beaten."

"No," said Hester; "it is *you* that have conquered."

Elsie smiled grimly. She lay silent; all at once her face changed. "Send for Ben," she whispered.

But when Ben came she was too ill to speak to him. There was hurrying outside where the colt was being led into the shafts of the lightest buggy to go for the doctor.

A JEALOUS WOMAN

Within Susan and Hulda stepped softly, and Ben turned to Hester with no thought of the strangeness of her presence. "She's so patient," he said; "she always was."

Elsie opened her eyes. "I made plenty of fuss, Ben," she gasped, "but not about pain." There was a different quality in her voice; it was hoarse and dry and small, as if it came from a distance. Her features had sharpened. Susan Pierce, who was in the room, turned away and threw her apron over her face.

"Why, if that isn't Susan, and she's crying," said Elsie. "Is—that—it? I guess it must be, for I don't seem to mind any more, Hester. Ben, I give you back your promise. And the will—send after it quick; I want to destroy it. Send after it quick!"

But after these few words she lapsed into a lethargy from which the doctor could not rouse her.

The moments of her life dwindled. The doctor, with professional calm, sat in the shadow, narrowly watching the patient, yet his thoughts involuntarily straying to the chance of his election to the vacant chair in the medical department. Susan and Hulda watched quietly in the hall. Hester sat on one side of the bed, and Ben on the other; and to neither did it seem strange that they should be keeping this darkling watch together. Ben supported his wife against his breast and fanned her. What visions of his wrecked married life, of the poisoned happiness, the worse than useless devotion, the strife and the heartbreak, were drifting in formless pictures before his hot eyes, who shall tell! At times, his lip quivered, and he kissed her hand.

There was the noise of horse's hoofs and the rattle of wheels in the yard.

Elsie opened her eyes. "Susan," said she, "don't cry. I didn't think you minded." Her voice was fainter; she paused between the words. "I was so —busy—with Ben—I —didn't think—I *missed* other things." She leaned her head closer to her husband.

"Is that the lawyer? Destroy—the—will. Hester, you're right. If you — bend closer, Ben, I want to whisper—" She whispered it in his ears. "If you want—to— marry Sadie—"

A JEALOUS WOMAN

"That little fool!" cried Ben, "*never!* Oh, darling, don't think of her!"

Dying as she was, Elsie smiled. "Oh, I'm so happy!" she sighed. She never spoke again. The lawyer, who was already on the threshold, advanced, saying: "You wish me to destroy the will, Mrs. Rogers?" but she only smiled and stirred her head a little on her husband's breast, like a child nestling its head for an easier sleep. "Don't disturb her," said Ben, sternly.

"I think, if there is anything of importance," began the doctor, after a single glance, "now—"

"*No*," said Ben. He bent to whisper in her ear; his tears dropped on her face.

She smiled again, with a little soft, shivering sigh, and was still.

The clock ticked in the hall. The lawyer stood in the doorway, the yellow envelope in his hand; and out under the eaves a thrush was pouring a wealth of joyous melody from his tiny throat. The doctor stepped gently to the side of the husband and wife. His eyes met Hester's. She rose and motioned to the others to leave the room.

"I'm sorry to intrude on you, Mr. Rogers," said the lawyer—it was half an hour later and they were sitting in the little parlor below—"but there are Mrs. Rogers's instructions regarding the will. It is a question—"

"There is no question. Let my wife's will stand."

"Perhaps you would like to know the provisions. I fancy they will not be objectionable to you. After a few small legacies to servants, she leaves you her entire estate on condition that you do not marry any one—other than Miss Hester Morrill, who appears to be a valued friend."

Ben did not answer; but at that moment Elsie need not have feared to read his heart.

A Problem in Honor

THE doctor's boy caught Miss Conway's surrey in the West End and handed Mrs. Reynolds' note to her. Miss Conway read it. There were only a few lines hastily scratched with a lead pencil on a card and pushed into an envelope. They ran:

"Dear Peggy:—My brother feels worse and is very anxious to see you; I am afraid the end is near, but perhaps not—it is so hard to tell.
"Ann."

"Tell Mrs. Reynolds I will be there at once, as fast as we can drive," said Miss Conway; and the doctor's boy sped away on his wheel. "To Mr. Wainwright's," she added to the coachman, who touched the horse lightly with the whip.

The coachman was a handsome young Irishman, smartly although soberly dressed in a plum-colored livery exactly matching the lining and body of the carriage. He wore no glaring pomp of white doeskin and top boots, but his coat fitted perfectly and his shoes and his linen were speckless.

The lady who sat in the carriage might be thirty-five or she might be forty-five. She was undeniably handsome; indeed, for her graceful and gentle charm, beautiful might seem a truer as well as a kinder word. She kept the girlish slenderness of her figure; her smooth, pale olive skin only showed her years in a few faint lines at the corners of her dark eyes and in her low forehead. Her hair was a very lovely gray. She was a great lady in the little city, and several ragged boys and girls came out from the bakery and gazed upon her admiringly. Two boys joined them presently; and the boys grinned. They had no admiration in their grin; but rather what one critic of human nature is pleased to call the savage emotion of humor.

The West End of Fairport is not a fashionable quarter. The shops are small and there is an undue proportion of saloons. One of these was opposite the carriage. It was of brick with a wooden façade, which was

A PROBLEM IN HONOR

painted a vivid crimson. In the doorway appeared a white-aproned barkeeper with elaborately smoothed hair scalloped over his forehead, and a shabby man in wrinkled clothes. These, also, were grinning. They stepped to one side and the red door framed several more faces—all a-grin.

The surrey remained in the same spot. That was the cause of the universal hilarity on the street. Doolan, the coachman, struck the horse again, this time sharply, although he knew that Miss Conway hated him to raise the whip.

The horse slightly heaved his flanks. It was a motion in a horse that might be compared to a shrug of the shoulders in a man. But he did not stir. He was a powerful bay, having a glossy skin and a restless eye. Miss Conway had bought him (at a great bargain) the week before. Doolan had engineered the trade. Up to this hour he had been proud of his horse; but now he was assailed by a darksome fear. He tried new tactics. He made an encouraging chirrup with his lips, and said "Sam!" encouragingly. But Sam merely braced his forelegs and rolled his eyes back on his blinders with their shining silver C, and took a fresh hold on his bit.

"Horse balky?" inquired the barkeeper, cheerful and interested.

"He's a bit narvous and high-spirited," answered Doolan, stiff and dignified.

"You *must* make him go, Doolan," cried Miss Conway, "even if you have to whip him!"

Doolan's blow had good will in it; but Sam only sagged his head. Doolan struck again and harder. With an indescribable expression of patient martyrdom Sam took the blow and did not move.

"He *is* balky," muttered Doolan.

"I had a balky horse, once," the barkeeper observed, the crowd by this time being enlarged by four more men, and two women in plain, scant, short skirts, basques of an antique cut and checked aprons. The latter housewives came from their domestic tasks in the rear of the shops and wore no bonnets. They looked sympathetically at the lady in the surrey and said "*Ach Himmel!*" and repressed the merriment of the boys.

A PROBLEM IN HONOR

"Vat did you done to your balky hoss?" one of the women said to the barkeeper. The crowd hung on his answer; Miss Conway leaned a little forward.

"I sold him," said the barkeeper, with the effect of making a joke.

"You git out!" reproved the wrinkled man, "you don't know nothing 'bout hosses. Young feller, you jump down and lead the critter a bit; and he'll go all right."

Doolan cast an oblique glance of scorn at the adviser and did not move.

Neither did Sam.

"Lady," continued the wrinkled man, "you tell that smart Alick to git out and lead the hoss—"

"With his head blinded!"

"No, jest his head kept so he can't move!"

"Build a fire under the wagon, he'll be glad enough to go then!"

"Say, Missis! lemme try my nigger chaser on him; I'll git him running!"

These different suggestions were fired from the crowd in almost simultaneous fusillade. Miss Conway looked anxiously at the horse; she said something to Doolan, who handed her the reins and got down scowling, ironically cheered by the boys. But although he went to the horse's head and told Sam, "Good Sam, good old boy—*you dom divil!*" to move on, there was no persuading Sam. Then the coachman set his teeth, sprang back into his seat and caught up the whip. Only one blow reached the horse before Miss Conway touched his arm.

"Don't do that," she said, quite calmly, "I've seen balky horses before; look at his ears! The next blow you strike him, he'll kick the dashboard to splinters!"

"You're right, lady, he will that," cried the barkeeper. "I'd a buggy smashed by a hoss looked like that one's twin brother. I built a fire under that hoss one day and he moved jest far 'nuff to set the wagon afire. *I* say unhitch him and maybe that'll fool him."

"I saw a dandy thing in a newspaper, dead sure for balky hosses," a man in the crowd offered; "it had reformed more balky horses than any remedy they'd tried in that town for a year." (The crowd showed signs of interest; Miss Conway looked at the speaker.)

A PROBLEM IN HONOR

"I wisht to goodness I could remember it! Queer I can't. It was a real simple thing."

Miss Conway was desperate. "I *must* get on," she said, almost imploringly to the crowd, "I'm just summoned to a—a dying friend. Doolan, I'm going to get out myself and try."

"Maybe so you vas to gif him some nice grass," one of the women suggested. "I go git you some. You valk ahead und he coom after till he git by dis blace und den he go all right. You see!"

But the gentle homeopathic remedy of grass tendered by his mistress in person, proved as useless as Doolan's heroic medicines of whip and voice. Sam hung his head. He looked as if he wanted—if such a thing may be said of a horse—to burst into tears; but he did not take a step toward the tempter. Miss Conway threw the grass to the ground, and looked at the horse.

"I'll give yous five dollars for him, lady, just as he stands; he ain't worth a cent more!" shouted a heartless boy. But the barkeeper took him violently by the ear and asked him, "Didn't you hear the lady say *why* she was in a hurry, you little—?" At which between pain and fright the boy began to whimper and Miss Conway instantly appealed for mercy. So the lad was released. Meanwhile Sam craned his neck forward, and being unhampered by any bearing rein, which Miss Conway (who had distributed at her own charges no less than fifty copies of *Black Beauty* among the different stables private and public in the town) considered to be wickedly cruel, he was able to nibble the bulk of the bribe that he had disdained, without moving a leg. Then, refreshed, he turned his pensive, mild eyes on Miss Conway. She was standing in the dust, the pretty yellow chrysanthemums of her filmy gown shifting about her in the wind, uncomfortably warm with her exertions, her dainty white hat blown to one side, and the white Chuddah shawl that she carried, fluttering from her arm.

Sam apparently thought well of her looks, for he rubbed his head against her shoulder with a little contented—or was it complacent?—whinney. Miss Conway's eyes flashed. With a sudden movement she

A PROBLEM IN HONOR

wound the shawl about the beast's head and bent over the place where his ear was wriggling, holding the head steady with both hands. "If you don't go I'll sell you to-morrow!" she called in his ear, and tugged at the bit.

Now, whether the unusual attack disconcerted the firm soul of Sam so that, in an amaze and vacillation of mind such as is known to undermine the strongest spirits when assailed unaware, he weakened in his intent, or whether he simply had stood as long as he wished and was now ready to go on again, it is certain that Sam allowed himself to be led a block; and that at the end of his walk, Miss Conway having removed the shawl and stepped into the surrey, he instantly trotted off briskly and virtuously, his head in the air and his eyes forward.

Miss Conway drew a long sigh. "What a horse, Doolan!" she exclaimed, "but we didn't lose much time, did we?"

"He's a fright!" said Doolan, "but no, Miss, not twinty minutes."

They had, however, lost twenty-five minutes; and twenty-five minutes to an irritable hypochondriac who, after fancying himself dying for twenty years, is dying in grim earnest at last, is a weary long time.

Wainwright had received the message sent by the doctor's boy, who unluckily liked to "scorch" and seized upon this admirable excuse to whirl back to the Wainwright house at a breakneck speed. Wainwright lived in an old-fashioned square brick house with a wooden cupola, and a narrow piazza supported by slender pillars running on three sides of the house. The house, which had been built when the town was new by one of the pioneers and later bought by Wainwright, stood in the center of a lawn covering half the block. Wainwright's own chamber looked out on the street and his bed faced the window. Therefore he saw the boy rolling down the gravel, hunched over his handlebar and chewing gum as he rode. A dull resentment seized him.

"Tell that little devil to come up here, into this room," said Wainwright.

He spoke sharply, although a minute before he had whispered his wishes.

A PROBLEM IN HONOR

The boy was heard shuffling through the hall, clattering up-stairs.

He was shown into the room by the nurse, a professional nurse brought from the hospital, who viewed him so coldly that he grew embarrassed. He stared about the room, comfortably but tastelessly furnished in the florid and heavy fashion of the black-walnut age. At last his eyes drifted to the great black bed, the carved top of which nodded its clumsy arabesques and rosebuds within a scant foot of the ceiling; and thence sank to the gray face on the pillows. He was staring at it when the eyes unclosed.

"Miss Gass, will you fetch me my purse,"—the boy watched the thin lips part and speak painfully; he looked awed.

"Take a five-dollar bill out of it." The boy had some difficulty in breathing naturally.

"Did you find Miss Conway?"

"Yes, sir." The boy spoke in a small, scared voice.

"Did you tell her—give her the note?"

"Yes, sir. She said she'd come right away. She was in a carriage, out riding."

"I thought," said Mr. Wainwright, speaking more distinctly, and keeping his eyes, which were large in contrast with his hollow cheeks, fixed on the shrinking lad, "I thought I'd like to give this to the messenger if he did his duty." He paused and beckoned for the glass on the table, but he only pretended to drink, watching the boy over the rim. The boy looked a shade less solemn.

"Yes," said Wainwright, "I thought I'd give you this bill,"—he rubbed his finger and thumb over it and held it up the better for the boy to see,—"but when I saw you coming up the road to a dying man's house, chewing gum and not caring a rap for him or anything else but yourself, I concluded I'd give it to a little kinder-hearted person. That's all. You may go. Miss Gass, put the bill away."

The boy gasped, but he moved away without retort.

Wainwright leaned back on his pillow and smiled. He was deadly faint with the exertion, but he mustered strength to open his eyes and watch the boy wheel away out of the yard. At the gate he dismounted. Perhaps it was for the outlet of some boyish insult of gesture which he knew the sick man could see, for he turned and looked up at the window: but he must have had a streak of rough chivalry about him; he looked, lifted his cap and flung himself lightly on his wheel.

"A pretty disappointed boy, *I* guess," said Wainwright.

The nurse made no comment; but she looked at the handsome, haggard face on the pillow and thought her own thoughts. To judge from the curl on her lip they were not approving.

Little Wainwright would have cared had he read her criticisms. He was busy thinking of his money. He had thought of his money for thirty-five years. He had scraped it together, dollar by dollar at first, then by the tens and the hundreds, later by the hundreds and thousands. When he was a boy he had vowed to make a fortune. Well, he had made it. Half a million was a big lump of money for a country town! He had said he would do it and he had done it. He had done most of the things that he said he would do. Except—yes, he hadn't married Margaret Conway. Did he really want the woman, or had he only kept up the chase all these years simply because she was the only thing that he had determined to have and had not secured? But he might, even yet—why didn't the woman come, d—— her? He lost his thought, so great was his weakness, but his will whipped his brain back to it, his last scheme. There was Ann: how many times had he felt a dull hatred of Ann, whom Peggy loved so ridiculously while she would not love him! Now he would win her through her love for Ann. Not one penny should Ann have unless Peggy yielded. But then—he *would* think it out—what was he asking so much of Peggy? To give her his name, a good name, good as hers if she didn't think so, to make her a dignified married woman instead of an old maid. And the money, too! And she would be his widow in a few days probably. How could any sane old maid object?

But why didn't she come? He grew

feverish, his nurse wrote in her little book and watched him furtively. He in his turn felt the instinct of concealment that comes to the sick so often, and pretended to sleep. But all the while he grew more and more impatient with Margaret Conway, all the while his flagging wit struggled to plan. But for that jibing horse he might have been more merciful. So well as he knew how to love he had loved Margaret; and but for the irritating delay his heart might have gone back to softer and kinder memories; and he might—such thoughts had come to him—he might have yearned to have her gratitude, her kindly memories of him: as it was, his imperious hatred of defeat was chafed to the raw by disappointment and irritating fancies of her carelessness and indifference to his state.

When the nurse finally announced, "She's come, Mr. Wainwright, she came up the side street," he was in his worst mood.

"You send over for Mrs. Reynolds; I want her, too," he said.

"Mrs. Reynolds is down-stairs."

"Then have her come up, too; I want

them both together. You go down yourself; it won't take a minute. Oh, I'm better; I shan't die while you're out of the room. Give me my box and my key and you go down."

Unwillingly the nurse went.

Ann Reynolds was Wainwright's half sister. Wainwright was eighteen years older than Ann. Their father was one of the pioneers of the town who came to the Mississippi just as the Indians were sullenly retreating from their hunting grounds. He built the first flour mill in the town and the first church. He came from Massachusetts, a true Puritan, grim, pious, rugged, indomitably industrious, careful almost to niggardliness in the daily conduct of his business, but capable of spending lavishly on occasion. Thus, during the later years of his life he built him a mansion on the principal street of the town, of a size and pomp (for those simple days) so striking that the gossips named it Wainwright's Folly. The great panic of '57 struck the town before the hammers were out of the house, and came near to justifying the nickname.

A PROBLEM IN HONOR

Perhaps, had he lived, Judge Wainwright (he was judge, mayor, state senator, banker and a colonel in the militia, playing many parts on his small stage) would have steered his fortune safely through the storm, but he died at the most critical moment and his son's credit was not that of his father; hence there was an enormous shrinkage in the property left behind. The rich man of the town left only an inconsiderable estate when all claims were paid. By a will made when he believed himself to be rich, he left all his estate for life to his widow, his second wife. After her death it was to be divided equally among the children. She was also charged with the payment of some legacies to the church and certain charities, further impairing the estate.

The first Mrs. Wainwright had been a woman of strong although curiously warped mind, in whose family, dimming its pride and public honor, was a black tradition of insanity. Born a gentlewoman and reared in luxury, there was no more insatiable worker, no keener saver in the pioneer community than she. She was a far famed house-wife, a nurse who traveled miles to lend her medical skill, and with it all she found time to read and to educate her children. But she had lapses of strange melancholy, during which she performed duties like one in a dream, faithfully but without zest.

Her husband respected her, admired her, and possibly, strong man though he was, a little feared her. Her children had the same mixture of feelings, with a predominance of the fear.

The second Mrs. Wainwright was a very pretty, delicate, obedient woman who played classical music and did not know how to cook. Her husband loved her devotedly, and often at the old settlers' gatherings at the county fair, the old story would be repeated how Judge Wainwright drove across the Mississippi on floating ice to get a cook for his wife, by this peril leaving two other pursuers of the gifted cook a night behind, since the river was frozen by morning, and they also crossed—but meanwhile the cook had been taken to Mrs. Wainwright.

There were six children—Peter and his sister Dorcas, who was married and lived in the town, children of the first Mrs. Wainwright; Ann, and three little brothers, the second Mrs. Wainwright's children. Peter felt sore and angry over the will. He was just beginning business, and he had a heavy load to carry. Nevertheless, he bought the house of the estate on easy payments, and he managed the money judiciously. He was the real head of the household for the next ten years. It must be confessed that he was rather a hard one, not hesitating to give the boys a sound hiding if they disobeyed him, and boxing Ann's ears if she interferred. But he did save the roof over their heads. He nourished the estate, he pared their living expenses to the bone, he worked early and late, and when Mrs. Wainwright, rather glad to go, slipped out of the world into the family lot, where she would not be reprimanded for having the piano tuned, or be obliged to turn little clothes, double the original property was distributed among the four heirs. Only four it was now, for two of the boys had died. The third boy died the year following, and then Ann married

A PROBLEM IN HONOR

Jacob Reynolds, a widower with four children. She married him, making no professions of an affection beyond decent regard. Two of his children were married, prosperous young men out of town—one in the far West, the other in Chicago. At home was a boy, an invalid from his babyhood, and the eldest daughter, who was reputed to have a will of her own.

Jacob Reynolds was a good fellow, quiet and kind and of moderate success as a merchant. He was not a brilliant match; but Ann was a plain, quiet girl who had inherited her father's harsh features as well as her mother's beautiful complexion. She inclined to stoutness in figure, starve and exercise as she might. It was not to be expected that such a girl would be able to marry at all. Most people considered Ann to be doing a wise thing. They would have been surprised to know that Ann had moments of suffering and absolute terror at the thought of what she had promised; or that she had promised more because of her pity for the crippled child and her weariness of her own hard and narrow life than anything else. Peter was

A PROBLEM IN HONOR

not especially moved by the deaths of the little boys; he grew impatient at Ann's "everlasting moping"; and he was angry to the point of rage when she announced her betrothal. Already the foundations were laid for his fortune. He didn't wish to marry—at present; he did wish an orderly, comfortable, frugally luxurious home, where special dishes could be prepared for him alone, and gas never burned in an empty room, and there were no servants (except the weekly washerwoman) to scatter prodigally.

However, Ann, who had moments of obstinacy (didn't she insist on giving the washerwoman meat at both meals and absolutely refuse to portion out the soap?) had a moment, now. She even took her miserable little fifteen thousand out of his hands and let Reynolds have it in the business. It served her right, Peter thought, that two years later, when Reynolds died suddenly (he was drowned at a picnic trying to save a child that fell overboard from an excursion steamboat), the business should be in bad shape and eventually some of the money should be lost. Mrs. Reynolds had enough left, however, to be able to keep her house and to live without asking help of her brother.

The invalid boy died, but the girl with a will of her own lived on, and no man ventured to seek her. In fact, there was a rumor that Patience (her unfortunately misplaced name), when excited, "threw things." One of the maids said that she could live forever with Mrs. Reynolds; but that there was no pleasing Miss Patty and she was " 'fraid for her life with her."

But for "the terrible Patience," as Miss Conway called Patty in secret, the two friends would have lived together. They had been friends ever since Miss Conway came with her father to the town more than twenty years ago. Why a brilliant, handsome, rich young girl like Margaret Conway should be so attracted by a plain young matron who had so few charms of face and manner as Ann Reynolds, was a subject of wonderment at first; but the wonder lessened in time. Mrs. Reynolds made a position of her own. She was not rich, nor pretty, nor fascinating, nor even of a picturesque piety; but little by little her acquaintances began to find that Mrs. Reynolds had an even temper and that useful if not shining quality which in a man is called "horse-sense." She was a woman that very many people liked. They called her a cold woman, but the critics would add, "There's nothing false about her."

It was in the first year of her coming to the town that Peter asked Margaret Conway to marry him. He had asked her many times since. The last time was when her father died, five years ago. She thought of it, to-day; and Ann, who was with her, thought of it also, for since that day Margaret had not met Peter except casually on the street.

The two women entered together. Peter's dull eyes, which had been of the keenest, traveled from his sister's sturdy figure, to which age and her sober clothing had given a sort of dignity in default of the grace which was forever beyond it, to the beautiful shape in the shimmering yellow flowered gown. Mrs. Reynold's features were almost fine now, softened by her gray hair; but they had none of the soft loveliness of the other woman's broad, low brow and oval cheek and exquisite mouth.

"I'll make Ann help me for once," he thought, grimly; "what makes Peggy so besotted with her anyhow?"

But that was not his affair. He held out his hand and very faintly smiled. His sister, guessing his wish, fell back behind Miss Conway, that he might take her hand first.

He had not been a good brother to her; but she looked at him lying with the shadow of the dread mystery that we all must meet, on his pinched face, and awe and pity chased every other feeling away. Perhaps his health excused his temper and his lonely unsatisfied life his greed. Poor Peter, he had loved Peggy, then, and he wanted to bid her good-bye! Ann, whom her world esteemed a cold woman, felt her throat contract and her eyes smart with the pity of it all.

She saw Peggy take his hand and the clawlike fingers close on her white, smooth hand. He smiled. "I thought you weren't

A PROBLEM IN HONOR

going to come," said he. His voice was a whisper.

"I came as fast as I could," said she, "I was delayed."

"Oh, I guess it's all right now you've got here. Peggy—do you mind my calling you Peggy?"

"Not now—not here—call me anything you like, that gives you—"

She had it on her lips to say "comfort," but there was something so presuming in taking it for granted that her presence or her kindness would be a comfort to a lover who had not made a sign for five years, that the sentence hung in mid-air and she finished it with an ambiguous smile.

"Peggy, you know—say, is that nurse woman here?"

The nurse moved into his sight with professional gentleness and her professional smile.

"I wish you'd go down-stairs and stay there until I send you word to come up," said Wainwright.

The nurse murmured something about the doctor's orders.

A PROBLEM IN HONOR

"There'll be a new doctor to order, if you don't," Wainwright retorted; "I've got something to say to these ladies in private."

The nurse hesitated, then she said: "Very well, sir. You take the responsibility of any excitement. Shall I fetch the ladies some chairs first?"

"No," snapped Wainwright, "they can get their own chairs. Now, Ann, you look out of that door"—the nurse had gone, still gentle but with disapproval bristling in every stiff line of her back—"see she isn't peeking and prying somewhere! Give me a sip of that whisky."

He eyed the cutting on the tumbler and marked the height of the liquid after he had drunk. "Hum," he sniffed, "nobody'll take any of that without me knowing."

"You needn't be afraid of Miss Gass taking any," began his sister, a little shocked.

"That's all right," he interrupted, "I'm suspecting no one, but there's no harm in keeping track of liquor. That's fine stuff. Pat sent it to me. Pat's a fool! Peggy!"

There was something painful and rasping about his voice; he spoke breathlessly, as if some inner, strong impulse pushed his words out of exhausted lungs.

"Yes," said Miss Conway.

"You know how long I've wanted to marry you?"

"Yes," said Miss Conway, again; but it was in a different tone.

"I want to marry you, now. No"—as her cheek burned and she opened her lips—"wait, you wait! I'll put it as a business proposition. I can't last two days. You'd only be my wife two days—that's nothing—just look after me a little—I won't be troublesome. Nurse will take care of me—you won't have to—just sit around a little so I can see you. And—no, don't speak yet!—I've made my will"—he fumbled in the box and painfully lifted out a paper in an envelope—"you read that"—he unfolded it and dropped it on the bed—"that's not the one. That gives everything to found a—a —never mind, that's if you won't do what I want—here—*here*—take it out!"

He was trembling with eagerness; he

gasped hideously for breath, but his eyes rolled on Ann, who would have summoned assistance. "No, just you two—whisky!"

The whisky revived him. He unfolded another paper and read: "To my beloved wife, Margaret Conway Wainwright, and my sister Ann Wainwright Reynolds—residuary legatees, share and share alike—that's what you'd like, isn't it? Marry me and the minute we're married I'll sign it. You want to make Ann comfortable—rich—there's two hundred and fifty thousand and up, apiece! Marry me, she gets it. Don't, and she—*does not get one penny!*"

Margaret Conway caught her breath. Her indignation rose, but she looked at her friend. Was the man in earnest or had his mind gone? And there was Ann, too proud to be helped by her as it was, but in this odious way she could—

"Oh, you ask a *wicked* thing!" she cried, passionately.

"Where's the wicked? It—it isn't as if I was going to live!"

"You make—a—a mock of the sacredest, the solemnest—sacrament. You ask me to

A PROBLEM IN HONOR

swear to love and honor and obey you when you know—"

"You needn't have an Episcopal clergyman and say all that; I'm not—particular—have a justice of the peace! But—don't cheat Ann out of two hundred and fifty thousand dol—"

"Oh, Annie, what shall I do?" cried Miss Conway, suddenly turning on her friend.

"If *you* say so—"

It was what Wainwright had expected, it was the contingency for the sake of which he had kept Ann in the room. His lips relaxed into the feeblest, strangest of smiles. Ann was very white.

"There is something you haven't counted in, Peter," she said, in a very quiet voice; "the doctor told me this morning that there was a bare chance of your recovery—"

He interrupted her with a scream of rage. "There isn't! there isn't!" he shrieked. "Ann, go down-stairs! call Miss Gass!"

He clutched Miss Conway's hand and rolled his head over on her arm, writhing. Mrs. Reynolds really feared that he would have a paroxysm and die then and there; she

A PROBLEM IN HONOR

obeyed him as rapidly as she could. The instant she was gone, however, he turned a white, wolfishly eager face on Margaret.

"Don't believe her," he pleaded, "it isn't true. Promise, promise!"

"I can't promise"—Margaret began; but the awful change in his face stopped her.

"I guess it has come—well, Ann won't get a cent, that's one good thing," he gasped.

He rolled off her arm and the crumpled wills lay on the bed before her.

Then the meaning of it all came to her as the lightning strikes and sears.

She had been bending over him; but she leaped to her feet. Her eyes blazed into his. "Oh, don't do it!" she begged. "*Peter*, don't do it! let me burn this wicked will—just nod your head. There's a piece of paper in the grate—and matches! Peter, dear Peter, say you won't punish Ann for my fault! You know that—that there was some one that I loved and he loved me and we couldn't marry. I'm *sorry* for you, Peter; won't you make me like to think of you and regret you and feel kindly—and affectionately to you? *Please* let me burn the will!"

"*No!*" said Wainwright; he thought that she would yield.

"Then I'll do it, anyhow!" she flashed back at him, and took two steps to the grate with the paper in her hand. She scratched the match; and the same second he made a supreme effort to rise in bed, stretched forth his hand and fell back with a groan.

"I've killed him," thought Peggy; but she lit the paper in half a dozen places and watched it blaze high before she ran to his side and raised him tenderly and put the whisky to his lips. But he could not swallow.

"I've killed him!" she thought, again.

Yet even with the thought, her eyes darted over to the grate and the lean brown triangles spreading downward under the flames, eating the closely written lines. She poured the whisky with frantic haste over his lips, and it trickled hideously down the corners of his mouth; she forced a few drops between his teeth; but she did not make a motion toward the bell to summon help until the blazing sheets were only a heap of light, black ashes. Then she rang. Already, however, Mrs. Reynolds and the nurse were in the hall. They came into the room before her fingers left the bell. The nurse pursed her lips and almost imperceptibly nodded her head. She was too well trained to say "I told you so!" but outraged talent must have some vent for its scorn. Instantly she had her hypodermic syringe out and into the whisky glass, and having charged it, bared Wainwright's arm and ran the tiny needle into the flesh, making each motion with an extraordinary rapidity and certitude.

"He was talking to me, and he had this attack suddenly," said Miss Conway, "and I'm afraid—"

"Heart, of course," said the nurse, not interrupting Miss Conway, whose words had died away unfinished; "there was always the danger. You fan him, please. There ought to be a reaction. Yes."

Wainwright had opened his eyes. He looked feebly from his sister, who was fanning him, to Miss Conway; he tried to move his hand. Margaret took it in hers; her own eyes sank into his, which had a strange, dull, peaceful, solemn expression, while hers were filled with entreaty and pain.

"You won't mind, Peter?" she said; "it will be all right?"

He did not speak; he did not even try to speak; only there was a light quiver of the fingers loosely clasping hers, and he turned his head very slightly and coughed. The nurse bent over him. Then she gently disengaged Margaret's hand.

"You ladies better go now," said she.

"He isn't——"

"Yes," said the nurse, "we can't do anything more for him."

She spoke in a subdued tone, without emotion. She knew Wainwright (and had known him during years) as a peevish and selfish invalid, slowly petting and pampering imaginary diseases into real, and as difficult a man about a bargain as she ever had met. But if she had little respect for the dead man, she had a professional quietude in the presence of death.

"I suppose you'll telephone Mr. Butler and he'll see about the arrangements," she continued.

Mrs. Reynolds nodded. She looked at the box on the bed and the one paper beside it, slipped to one side of the blanket; she did not look at the grate, but with a curious light on her face slipped her arm through Margaret's and led her from the room.

"Wait," she said in the hall; "I must attend to Pat, first."

The grim details which wait insistently on death and make no account either of grief or the indifference that is sadder than grief, demanded their hour; and Peggy helped her friend where she could.

Pat Butler came at once. He was the only other near relative of the dead man, the son of his sister who had died when the boy was born. It had been supposed that Wainwright would leave him the bulk of his fortune, as he showed him some gleams of human interest, and used to have him stay in the house; but within the last six months there had been a quarrel between the two men (of what nature they kept

A PROBLEM IN HONOR

strictly to themselves), and apparently a complete breach.

Pat had lived more with his aunt than with any one else; and she was as fond of him as of a son. And next to his aunt he both loved and admired Miss Conway, or, as he always called her, "Aunt Peggy."

Pat came into the hall, a little breathless—he had ridden on his wheel up the hill—a little flushed, but, as usual, not in the least overheated. He was not handsome; from his Irish father he inherited not only a sweet temper and high courage but a typical Irish nose, broad at the base, long Irish upper lip and red curls. To counterbalance this, he had a fine figure, a dimple in his cheek, a beautiful fair freckled skin, very white, short, even teeth and small but brilliant dark-blue eyes with thick eyelashes.

Pat had assumed a decent gravity of bearing, but he made no pretense of grief.

"It took me a little while to arrange things," said he, after he had kissed both women, "so I didn't get here quite so soon. I didn't think it would happen so soon. Doctor Barker said he might have an attack and go off in it any day, or he might live a month longer. And Sollers, who was called in consultation, you know, Aunt Peggy, said he might possibly rally and get over this and live for a year or two. These kidney diseases are so uncertain. Well, poor fellow, it wasn't to be!"

Peggy had turned pale at his last sentences: she stole a glance at Mrs. Reynolds.

"He seemed to be sure he was going to get over it," continued Pat, in a meditative way. He felt obliged to make some appropriate conversation in a house that was so mournfully not of mourning. "I was up here, yesterday, and saw him. But he got much worse at night, and when I called the nurse thought he wouldn't better see me. I offered to stay in the house all night; but the nurse thought it wasn't necessary. I suppose he had another seizure this morning. I was superintending a house" (Pat was an architect) "and I had arranged with the man next door, to get any telephone; but none came until yours. You were here in time?"

Mrs. Reynolds described the last scene

briefly, making no mention of Peggy's part in it, perhaps because of a warning pressure on the arm from Peggy herself, who had risen and stood behind her chair. She took the word.

"He grew worse," said she, "and Annie went down for the nurse, and I was alone with him—no, he asked Annie to go down; I think it was before he grew worse,"—a little red spot flickered in her cheek as she made the effort to be exact—"and he was talking to me. He—he grew excited, and all at once his face changed; I gave him the whisky, but he couldn't take it. Then the others came. But the hypodermic didn't more than rouse him. He never spoke."

Pat's bright eyes brightened with a sudden intelligence. But he had no comment.

"Isn't some one coming?" said Peggy. Pat instantly took the hint and went out into the hall to avoid the indecorum of the bell sounding. Peggy, who had known that he would go, caught her friend's arm, saying in a vibrating voice, "Annie, you must get up to the room and put the will in the box and the box away—"

"I have," said Mrs. Reynolds. "Peggy, did he have you burn one of those wills? Only the unsigned one was there. And I saw some charred paper in the grate. I thought it as well to take care of that."

Miss Conway's hazel eyes looked darker, for their dilated pupils; they gazed at Mrs. Reynold's middle-aged, common-place face with a curious tenderness.

"Yes, I burned the signed will," she said.

"But why did he want you to?" said Mrs. Reynolds. "Did he relent. Did he forgive you for refusing? You know why I spoke; it was because he might get well; it was not fair to you—"

"I am glad I refused; it was a wicked thing he asked me to do," said Peggy, "but I forgive him. Don't let's speak of it ever again."

Mrs. Reynolds' steady eyes, not beautiful and liquid, like the other eyes, but clear and frank, never moved from her friend's pale face. "I've got to understand, Peggy; please don't evade me. I thought we didn't conceal a thought from each other, dear."

Peggy unexpectedly smiled.

"I don't want to evade you, dearie," she said, and she sighed almost as if relieved, "but it seemed selfish not to take this on my own shoulders. But if you want me—no, he didn't relent. I begged him, I—I called him Peter and took his hand, I was as humble—but he said 'No'—like that. And then I told him I should burn it anyhow. And I did."

Mrs. Reynolds got up out of her chair. She did not spring, she rose deliberately as she always moved, and walked deliberately, a little heavily, to the window, where she stood looking out. Miss Conway, still standing by the chair, looked after her.

"Mind, I didn't want to tell you," said she, "but, since I have, I am going to speak out. He was a hard, cruel brother to you. He made a slave and a drudge of you all your girlhood. He never gave you a penny when you married—"

"He made me a present; I had my own money to buy my wedding things."

"He gave you a silver ice pitcher, plated. I have seen it often. And the plate didn't wear well. He never helped you; he has let you scrub along on narrow means while he has piled up his thousands buying farm mortgages and tax titles and charging high interest. He pretended to like Pat, and would take him away from you all he could and say mean things of you. Then, for some whim of his own, he quarreled with Pat and cut him out of his will. And I suppose he wanted to give every penny to some charity to spread his name abroad as a great benefactor and philanthropist. He wanted to defraud Pat and you. Now he can't. And I'm glad I made it so he can't. Pat and you will get everything."

Mrs. Reynolds did not stir. She was looking out of the window with knit brows. But she did not see the wide lawn and the tall maples that had been growing ever since her father died. She was trying to understand, to see her way.

"Annie," said Peggy, in a low tone, "Annie, you don't think I did wrong?"

Mrs. Reynolds checked a kind of laugh, rather a bitter laugh.

"Well, you know what you did was against the law."

"Why—yes, of course"—she threw back her beautiful head, her lips parted in a scornful smile—"it's a penitentiary offense, isn't it?"

"I don't know; speak lower. It's against the law."

"Well, it doesn't matter. Nobody will ever know. The law is a blundering sort of thing. That doesn't bother me. It's you. You seem to think I did wrong."

"Don't you think so?"

"Certainly I don't," responded Peggy, with some warmth; "you know how you are situated. You won't take money from me, although we have been more than sisters for twenty years almost. You won't come to live with me and be comfortable—we would be so happy, Annie—but you insist that so long as there is Patience and you haven't enough for her to board as she would like or to keep house, you must stay with her; and you won't let me try to put up with Patience. You who could do so much with money, have to calculate your car fare—"

"But you are always giving me money to give away!"

A PROBLEM IN HONOR

"You don't ask for half you would give, yourself. Well, you'll have plenty, now, Annie! Why don't you speak to me? You are not angry with me?"

The tears were in her eyes. Mrs. Reynolds crossed over to her—not deliberately, now, but swiftly, with a kind of fierceness in her rapid steps and the look on her face; and there was a touch of fierceness in the close embrace in which she crushed the supple, slender figure of her friend.

"My darling," she cried, "you can do anything you please. I shan't be angry with you. You are the best woman in the world, the sweetest, the dearest; and I love you better than anything in it, and Pat next to you, and you did it for us; but, dear, we can't take it!"

"You—can't—take it!" cried Peggy. She was crying softly in a nervous reaction from the strain of the last hours, but at the words she slipped out of her friend's arms and faced her.

"Don't you see, it's like—like stealing his money. He didn't give it to me. And it was his to give. He made it all. There wasn't enough to mention left by father; and he increased the estate so much before it was divided that he more than gave us back that. He had a right to do what he liked with his own. And he didn't mean to give it to me—or to Pat. I don't know what to do about Pat. He ought to know, and we ought to find out what the will said and do it with the money. But I can't tell Pat—"

"I don't in the least mind your telling Pat," interrupted Peggy; "he'll think as I do, I'm sure, and tell you you are crazy."

"May I tell him?" Mrs. Reynolds asked, eagerly.

Peggy assented, repeating what she had said before. And later in the day, after the somber bustle of the preparations was over, and the friends of Mrs. Reynolds and the official associates of the dead man (friends he seemed to have none) had come and made their offers, after the kindly fashion of a Western town, and gone their ways, and Ann and Pat sat in the dark parlor, with the noises of the street muffled by distance and the closed blinds, she repeated the story.

A PROBLEM IN HONOR

Pat made no comment until the very end. He jumped out of his chair and paced up and down the room.

"Well! wouldn't that kill you dead!" he remarked. Then he asked: "Is it perfectly safe? Nobody suspects anything?"

"It's absolutely safe. But what shall we do, Pat?"

"Do? Oh, there's only one thing to do. Follow his d—— skinflint will. It was his own money. He had a right to do what he chose with it. And Aunt Peggy threw it into the fire! And she can't see she did anything wrong! Mads the old man into a fit that kills him, and burns his will before his eyes, and goes home to say her prayers without a ripple! Well, give me a sweet, good, pious, womanly little woman to play smash with the commandments." He grinned, but Mrs. Reynolds answered with fire:

"Peggy is the best woman I know, Pat. Don't you remember how unfailingly sweet she was with old General Conway. I liked the old General, and he was Peggy's father, but he did have cranky whims; but she never seemed to know they were anything unreasonable. And you know why she never married. There was insanity in his family. Finally the young fellow himself saw the danger, and they parted, although it broke her heart. You don't know, though, that the weekly visit she used to make to Chicago for years was to see him—in the asylum where he had to pass the last years of his life. He died there ten years ago. And when she came home her father fell ill; and he wanted her every minute, and she never let him see her anything but cheerful.

"My poor girl! I remember how she once was alone with me for a few moments, and she began to cry and checked herself, saying: 'I never let myself cry in the daytime, because it's so hard to stop before it shows!' I used to walk past the house every morning at a certain time and she would come to the window. And I used to write her little notes to cheer her up; but it was so little I could do. Yet she never said one complaining word. I know she never thought one. And hasn't she been more than a mother to Mabel? You said yourself that Mabel was her very image and—"

"I'm awfully in love with Mabel, and mean to tell her so the minute I have enough money to make it decent," interrupted Pat. "Sure. But I'm not criticising Aunt Peggy. No, I only mean that Aunt Peggy is the old type of a good woman and you are the new. Aunt Peggy is just as conscientious as you, but your lights are different. See?"

"Not entirely, Patrick. I only see that we can't take Peter's money. Goodness knows I wish we could; but I should feel like a thief, and I should be one, too."

"That's the way I look at it," said Pat, rumpling his red curls; "there are some fundamental things underlying all creeds and all morality. And in a scientific age like this, up-to-date moralists try to get at those and let the non-essentials go. But the old woman isn't scientific; keep her within the beaten paths where she has been told all about the right and wrong of things and she'll go to the rack with a smile for her principles—that's Aunt Peggy. But give her a sudden dilemma in morality where she

A PROBLEM IN HONOR

has to blaze her own moral way, and I tell you her heart is going to handle the ax; and the ten commandments aren't in it!"

"She doesn't think about breaking the commandments—"

"Of course not. Neither do you if you are following them. You reason out the question on the line of fundamental morality. You don't consider the persons involved at all. She doesn't consider anything else. It's the old woman and the new. However, to get back to the question. We decide we must give the money to the object named in that confounded will. What was it?"

"He didn't tell us."

"And the will is burned. But some lawyer must have drawn it up."

"Carpenter and Bates drew it up. I went to see them this afternoon, knowing that they did things for him occasionally; and most lawyers, you know, have some other lawyer make a will—I suppose on the same principle that most doctors have another doctor called in when they fall ill. They had drawn it up. And he had it signed and witnessed in their office March 10th of this year, and they know of no later will—"

"But in favor of whom?" said Pat, impatiently, making a favorite gesture of his with his hands, opening them and waving them. "Who gets the money?"

"They didn't know; he left the place blank and filled it himself."

Pat whistled. Mrs. Reynolds put one knee over another, an attitude which she never allowed herself in public. "You see," she continued, "we shall have to reason it out. March 10th? that was the day after his quarrel with you. I think he made it because he was angry with you."

"Very likely," said Pat composedly; "it was one of his favorite amusements—making wills disinheriting me. He used to read them aloud to me and then put them away in his tin box. At first I would be furious; but I got so I used to laugh at him. I came to the conclusion he meant to trick me and leave all his property to a college, or a hospital, something that would take his name, and have a big picture of him hanging up in the hall. The last time we quarreled—

well, what do you suppose over? I didn't like to talk about it while he was alive, but I'm pretty cross, now, and don't mind talking. It was the Catholic church, no less. He knows I'm not much of a Catholic, and if you'll believe, he wanted me to join the Congregationalist church. Me! I didn't usually get cross; but I confess I told him I wasn't a hypocrite, and he was a cur to ask me to forsake the faith of my fathers, which I liked even if I didn't believe in every old thing about it. He told me I'd never see a dollar of his money, and I told him he might take his money to—humph, with him! I was nasty, that's true; and I acted like a chump to row with a sickly old sinner like him."

"Do you suppose he left his money to the Congregational church? They are very anxious to build, and they would name the church after him."

"That wouldn't take it all. It might take some. He used to tell me he thought the best monument a man could leave after him was a public park. He told me that a week before he died."

"But he had a quarrel with the city after

A PROBLEM IN HONOR

that, and swore he never would pay the pavement tax, and said he would move out of town," said Mrs. Reynolds.

"Yes, I remember," said Pat, gloomily, "and I remember, too, that he didn't like a sermon of the Congregational minister, and was going to go to the Episcopal church. What did he think of hospitals?"

"He never spoke of one to me. A fund for supplying every sick man with patent medicines would be more in his line. Do you remember how he used to buy every new nostrum?"

"He hadn't any old servants to pension off, for he was always changing. These came last month. And we're about all his kindred. I say, Aunt Ann, we are simply driven into sin. We've got either to keep that money for ourselves, or we have to give it away according to our own notions and we get the credit. I don't see any way out of it."

"Let us give it to the park, then; have it called by his name."

"But he was raging at the city."

"He was raging at everything, at us, at everybody."

Pat rose. He had settled his disquiet in a chair for the last ten minutes—he came up to his aunt.

"I have a queer sort of notion," said he; "let us go up-stairs, where he is, and talk of it before him. If there is such a thing as his being around, he ought to give us a tip."

Mrs. Reynolds agreed. She felt herself before a blind wall; and she did not dare to listen to her own judgment lest she should be selfish—wherein, perhaps, she showed herself a true daughter of generations of self-tormenting Puritans.

"You know Peggy is there?" she said, as she stood before the closed door.

She answered his look of astonishment. "Yes, she said that he would like her to be with him, his last night here."

"Well, I give up women," said Pat. "They're too deep for me."

Peggy was sitting quietly beside her old lover. The room was brightly lighted, and his uncovered face wore the look of infinite peace that is death's first merciful token. Peggy had her prayerbook in her hand. She looked sweet and calm, and Pat felt an awkward shame of his words down-stairs. And, then, as he stood nearer, he perceived that there were traces of tears on her cheeks.

"I have been thinking," said Peggy, her soft voice like a strain of music—"I have been thinking how sad it is for him to lie here with no one to shed a tear because he is dead. I could not help crying. As much, I suppose, as he cared for any one, he cared for me. I think he would like me to be here. And—you know, he did press my hand. I think he forgave me. Poor Peter!"

Pat gave a little gasp.

"I wish to God I knew what is right to do!" cried Mrs. Reynolds, with a sob. "Peter, what do you want us to do with your money? We'll do anything you say if we only knew!"

But Peggy laid her hand almost caressingly on the thin hands clasped above the quiet heart.

"I know what Peter wants," said she, "it has come to me, sitting here and praying. I don't think I did wrong to make Peter do right. He doesn't see things through a blur now; he would rather have our kindly, for-

A PROBLEM IN HONOR

giving thoughts and our gratitude than have you scatter the money. Give some of it away to something that will be called by his name and divide the rest between you."

"I don't know but she is right," said Pat.

"If you had only seen a line in the will to guide us," said Ann.

"I only saw the date," said Peggy, "January 3—"

"What!" screamed Mrs. Reynolds, "are you sure! January?"

"I am perfectly sure—but why?"

"They told me of that will. It gave everything to Pat. He must have destroyed the other will himself."

"By Jove, he was only using that will for a bluff," cried Pat.

"I know he destroyed one will," said Peggy, "not long before he died. Miss Gass told me. It was one of March 10th, she said. He told her the date. But, Annie, do you mean that will gave everything to Pat? Ought he—"

"No," cried Pat, putting his arm about her waist, "I'm the one to talk, now; you burned up my rights, Aunt Peggy, and for that you will say your best for me to Mabel to make me your own true nephew, and you will say nothing while we share the estate, Aunt Ann and I, and give Uncle Peter his memorial. Uncle Peter, isn't that right?"

And as Peter Wainwright's placid mask lay before them, almost seeming to assent, his old love suddenly bent and kissed his forehead.

"Poor Peter," she said, "you did forgive me. I know. And it will be all right."

On the Blank Side of the Wall

MARY, the laundress, brought the card to Margaret the cook for advice, it being the waitress's "afternoon out," and Mary herself new to the place and timid about the visiting list.

"She wants particularly to see Mrs. Darcy," explained Mary.

"Who is it?" said Margaret. "I got my hands in the bread. I do think folks oughtn't to come on days that ain't Mrs. Darcy's day, especially now we're in such trouble. I know Mrs. Darcy's got a lot of letters to write to-day."

"Shall I tell her Mrs. Darcy begs to be excused? Is that what you say?"

Mary took kindly to social forms. She felt that to live in a family which kept "three girls," a coachman in livery, and a boy to help about the stable was something to write her friends. It was a quiet, unpretentious Western city, and Mrs. Darcy's was considered a large establishment. Mary felt that she would have been much more elegant than Annie the waitress, who hated to "excuse" Mrs. Darcy and would blurt out a lie cheerfully—"She ain't to home, ma'am; I guess she must have gone out"—when she knew Mrs. Darcy was up-stairs in her sitting-room.

"No, you won't," said Margaret, grimly. "That's Miss Harmon's card"—she had looked at it extended by Mary—"and Miss Harmon and the Senator used to send over flowers 'most every day when Mr. Winthrop was sick. I know Mrs. Darcy'll see her. They say the Senator ain't going to git well, either. It'll come awful hard on her. There's jest them two, and they've been together so many years! What you a-waiting for?"

She sighed as Mary ran off. And she told Thompson the coachman, who came in for orders presently, "I hated to disturb her, but I knew she'd not refuse to see Miss Harmon."

BLANK SIDE OF THE WALL

Thompson said: "Kinder queer, her coming when her brother's so awful sick. It's bad about the Senator, ain't it? I was reading his resignation only last Sunday. He's got a deal to leave. They was talking of him for President, Mr. Win told me."

A tear shone in Margaret's honest eyes as she kneaded the bread harder. "And who knows but Mr. Win might have been the President himself if he'd a-lived? He was smart enough."

"Yes; he was smart," Thompson agreed, sadly. "And he was easy on hosses——"

"Well, I'm glad you admit that now, if it is too late, all the same. The way you'd go at that poor boy if a hoss was sweating in summer! I don't wonder your conscience is pricking, Richard Thompson!"

"Well, it ain't then," retorted Thompson, in no discomposure. "I didn't mean nothing serious, and he know'd I didn't, and he always laughed. He was a hearty laugher," added Thompson, with a little gulp. "I can hear him now!"

"So can I," said Margaret, and began to cry.

"There, now, Margaret," Thompson soothed her; "I can't say a word about him but you're all upset."

"I've known him ever since he was five years old," sobbed Margaret, "and he never give me a sassy word 'cept the time he took my fresh sponge cakes to give to two raggedy little dirty boys that said they hadn't had anything to eat for a week—little liars! And I run after him and snatched 'em away, and he threw all the rest of the cakes over to the boys, he was so mad, and called me a stingy old tomcat, and said I was crueler than Nero—the precious lamb!"— Margaret wiped her eyes on her wrist—"Oh, dear! He was such a sweet little boy! I remember how mad I was, too, for the cakes was for charlotte russes, and company coming and a big lunch, and we didn't have so much help as we do now, then. I told him jest how it was. 'And you needn't think I'm going to tattle on you to your mamma,' says I, 'for I ain't. I'm going to make another batch of cakes, but I ain't going to forgit how you treated me for one while!' Why, that poor little tenderhearted child he burst out crying, and what does he do but run off and get me every one of the eggs he was saving to hatch chickens. Well, I never expect to see another child like him! And he kept his sweet way with him after he growed up——"

"But you couldn't fool him worth a cent!" Thompson struck in. "Nor you couldn't scare him, neither! 'Member the time he went out on the river in the sailboat and they got tipped up, and he could swim like a fish but he wouldn't leave the other boy and held him on? And when they got ashore them two boys walked eight miles into town and telephoned so's his mother shouldn't be worried. And that Mr. Cane that was with him at college told me he seen him with his own eyes run into a house afire and git a woman out, and I know he could fight with his fists, for I've seen him. He got a prize at college for fighting, I know, too."

Margaret sighed in acquiescence: "He's just like his mother; just her sweet way."

"His pa was different, I heard," ventured Thompson.

BLANK SIDE OF THE WALL

"Jest as hard as nuts and sharp as a file," said Margaret, "and stick to things like pitch. But no doubt he was a good man. It was wonderful, though, the way Winthrop got all his mother's good ways, and all his father's, too. Oh! the poor woman, Richard! When I'm rebelling for myself I think of her. No other child but him, and her whole soul bound up in him like it was! How is she going to bear it? And think of the villains that's let to live!"

"That's right," said Thompson, meekly. "Well, if she ain't wanting the carriage I guess I'll go."

Up-stairs, Augusta Darcy sat before a heap of letters, her eyes wandering across the street. The Harmons' modest wooden house had a background of elms and great oak trees, but in front only a narrow yard held off the street. Mrs. Darcy could see clearly the piazza with the greening honeysuckle before the Senator's windows. His study was on the right hand. Often during those nights of watching which had seemed to her so ghastly in their sickening anxiety, but the worst of which she would welcome now, she had seen the Senator bending over his papers. There was a window garden in the study. To-day, she could see the Senator's nurse watering the Easter lilies.

The nurse had been head nurse at a hospital. She prided herself on her professional composure, but it could not restrain her furtive tears that black day when, almost without warning, hope let go its grasp and they knew Win must die. With a kind of gratitude the mother again saw the nurse, whose hours of duty were over, begging the doctor to let her stay through the night, while the tears rolled unchecked down her cheeks.

The woful cinematograph of those last days enacted itself again, as it had enacted itself every day, almost every hour, since her boy died. His face, as she watched it while the soul drifted away, was clearer to her eyes than the scene before her. She saw it change as a ripple changes water; she saw the placid, unrecognizing features settling into peace; she heard them trying to rouse him, to win a last look for her. She wished that they would not vex him.

All that she begged then was that he should pass in peace. But now her heart cried out for one farewell to remember instead of that unearthly content—that smile after he was dead!

Yet it was her only comfort. Sometimes she felt that she had seen the end, but sometimes it was as if his soul had waved a message of hope and meeting to her in that smile, before it went into the dark. If she could only know that he was somewhere—Win himself, not a "glorified spirit," or a different, unremembering soul, but Win, whose baby fingers had smoothed the pain out of her heart; the little, loving, velvet-cheeked, impetuous boy; the lad at school, not over-fond of study, but doggedly working to win prizes for his mother's vanity; the gallant young man who was her lover and comrade as well as her son—if she only knew that he was happy, how little her own desolation would matter! She looked out at the chill April sunshine, and felt it flooding his grave. Where was he? Was he anywhere?

Augusta Darcy was what may be called a

"supporting member" of the church. She was the largest contributor to the rector's salary; she was President of the Guild; she was a liberal giver and a reasonably constant church-goer. She had the greatest respect for religious things. And she often wondered whether anything that she heard was true.

This was not the first time that death had robbed her; it was not the first time that she had groped vainly in the deep places of her soul to find comfort. But, those times, when comfort had come, it had been through the slow healing of time, the gradual blurring of pain by other interests, other affections— never through any answer to her questions. And out of her sorrows she had brought with her a keener sympathy for all sorrow; a biting sense of the helplessness of love and a sick faintness of the soul before the impenetrable future.

This time she knew that there never could come to her interests or affections vivid enough to console. Through a young, strong, gentle soul that loved her she had been akin to youth and hope and the splendid rush of growing life. She had lost more than the darling of her heart—she had lost her interest in living. Something had snapped in her heart. It is grief that makes the soul grow old. Augusta had always been young—not merely "young for her age," but young in her joyous readiness for every new experience, her unquenchable hope. Her own people had a fine old name and a meager estate. Augusta had borne the discomforts of poverty with a gay and frank courage. When she had been menaced by what might prove to be a mortal disease she had not flinched.

"Glad did I live and gladly die; and I laid me down with a will," she quoted to the doctor when he told her the worst that was to be feared. And when the danger passed she was cheerful but not elated; assuredly not awed and grateful, as the doctor secretly thought that she should be.

But where was her courage now? Outwardly she was calm enough—she had been calm from the first. She had quietly taken up, one by one, the daily household habits which had been jostled aside by the unnatural life of the sickroom. She was a woman of the world; a woman with a position and a host of friends. She shirked nothing of the etiquette of grief; she acknowledged every courtesy in her own hand; to the friends and kindred near enough to express their sympathy she responded, thanking them in the fewest possible words, then talking of something else. She did not go to her club, but she attended an "important meeting" of the Guild, and her comments on the question at issue were quite in her old fashion. The women smiled, for she was not only distinctly to the point, but her shrewdness had a dash of humor. And she smiled, too. Yet she was thinking, "That would amuse Win; I can't tell it to him." And she was remembering, and she was saying to herself: "This it is to have a broken heart. You care for nothing—not even your own suffering. That's how you know there is no hope. If you were suffering so you wanted to scream that would be a paroxysm, and paroxysms, soul or body, pass! But this is like the pain of a mortal disease—not beyond endurance but beyond hope!"

From such thoughts her fancy slipped back to last summer—"O God! only last summer"—when they were in the Adirondacks and she broke her arm. The guide set it, they being miles from a doctor or an anæsthetic, and Win and his two college chums stood by, catching their breath. She did not so much as shiver. All the while she said to herself, "The pain's nasty, but it's outside—it isn't I." A thrill of happiness conquered the red-hot torture of the twists as she heard Tom Cain (the great half-back, and revered accordingly by Win,) whisper, "Oh! isn't she a thoroughbred?" She looked up to smile, cheering Win. "It's not bad, really; he does it so skillfully."

She knew that her boy was proud of her. It was delicious to have Win proud of her in a new way. Afterward, his soul overflowed. "Tom says he knows, now, how the French marquises looked on their way to the guillotine!" cried he. "They wore just that smile. You've made a mash of Tom, mother!"

Then she told him about her thought of the pain.

"Perhaps," said Win, thoughtfully, "that's the difference between mental and physical pain. Don't you remember how, when I cut my knee breaking into the conservatory, I whistled while the doctor probed for the glass and was greatly admired for my sand, as I very well knew—"

"Yes, dear; we both dearly like to be admired, you and I," said she. And their eyes met. Win's were dark, with long, black lashes, hers were violet, but the expression was the same. They both laughed.

"Dear!" said Win, patting her hand. Then he went on: "And don't you remember how, the minute I discovered that the injury would prevent my going to the circus, all my sand leaked out and I bawled like a calf? The first pain had only hurt my knee. But not going to the circus, my first circus, that loosened the very foundations of being!"

The light words returned to her. They were not light to her now. Yes; it was true—that foolish pain was not herself, but this ache of the heart was a hideous part of her very being. And by that token she knew that she could never rid herself of it. So long as she lived this cruel partner would keep step with her soul. "But I wouldn't mind it," she whispered; "I wouldn't mind it, dear, if I could know that you were somewhere and were happy!"

She did not know. She looked at the woodbine masking the drab front of the Harmon house. The tulips and lilies of the window garden swayed, and she remembered that behind their gay pomp a man lay, dying by inches.

"Poor Miss Harmon," she sighed, " she will have to wonder about it, too." She half smiled as she sighed in the kind of compassion not unmixed with amusement which some people always evoke. She was thinking of Miss Harmon at the club. Ten years ago she had become a member of Augusta's literary club. She was a neutral-tinted woman of small stature, modest demeanor and an unobtrusive and self-respecting dowdiness of garb. Viewing her, one saw at a glance that she bought the best of materials and was true to the dressmaker of her youth. The other salient features of her presence were a Roman nose, a nearsighted frown and a trick of blushing, which imparted to her elderly face a spectral girlhood. During all the ten years she never had made a speech, nor did she ever fail to second Mrs. Darcy's resolutions.

The papers which she read before the club were always described by the local journals as "containing an immense amount of study and thought." She read them in a hurried, agitated voice and looked ready to faint when she sat down. Once she had a severe cold, and Augusta, out of mere careless good nature, offered to read her paper. Augusta's voice (the light, flexible American voice, which can be as expressive as gray eyes) was mellowed by the Western climate, and had been carefully cultivated by good masters. She had, moreover, the dramatic gift and the magnetism of every good speaker. She read as if Miss Harmon's thoughts were her own, and the applause was great. Miss Harmon wiped her eyes. Every member present congratulated her later, and many of them congratulated the Senator.

"It was all Mrs. Darcy," said Miss Harmon.

It was from this time that the impression began to drift about the club that Miss Harmon had an extraordinary admiration for Mrs. Darcy. It was so diffident, however, that Augusta, who was usually ready enough to detect her followers, did not notice it until the glee club of Win's college sang in the town, and the Harmons took ten seats at the concert.

She was gracious to this humble admirer because it was her nature to be gracious, and she was grateful because the admirer never seemed to expect any intimacy.

During Win's sickness, flowers came from the Harmons almost daily, and daily the Harmons' one maid (they were not rich) went around to the kitchen door to inquire.

Miss Harmon explained to her friends: "I hate to send Katy, but I don't want to ring the bell myself and I don't feel free to run around back, so I just take the dishes while Katy goes."

Augusta told Win, and he laughed. "She's a right good sort," said he, "and I don't

BLANK SIDE OF THE WALL

like her any the less that she thinks the sun rises and sets in you, mother. It is good of her to think of me when she's in such trouble herself. You know I saw the Senator at the reception they gave him. He knew about it then, and I'd heard. It made me feel queer to see him and hear him. He told me a funny story, and I was thinking all the time how he knew he must give it up just as he had got his hand on it. But he's a real old sport. He never made a sign. I daresay it's worse for her, if anything, than for him, for she's always been with him. They pinched and scraped together and she has been his private secretary to save money. Now, just as he is famous and successful he has to go. Mother, there are some awfully cruel things in life."

"Yes," said Mrs. Darcy. He was so much better that they thought him out of danger, and he was eager to talk and to listen to her.

He went on: "Do you ever wonder what becomes of us when we die?"

Mrs. Darcy shivered. She who was

usually so ready, had not a word at her command. "Yes," she said somberly, "but I don't know."

"If we are immortal I suppose this one little patch of life cuts a very small figure, and our troubles here we think of just as a man remembers how desperate he was as a child over some fool little thing. Don't you know how I cried over the circus and wished I was dead because I had so many enemies? The doctor was the chief, and then poor grandma; but I excepted you because I saw you were almost as mournful as I. Now maybe it will be that way in some other existence. All I remember now is how nice you were to me, and that always will be present, but all the bad part is a joke. Maybe our bad quarters of an hour will be like that—all the pain gone, but all the—the love"—he said the word with a boy's shyness at any deep feeling—"left. I wonder how Harmon feels about it all. It's queer, but I wish I could see him!"

Augusta recalled the talk to-day. She had never cared for Senator Harmon, a rough-hewn old Spartan, who was called "a man of the plain people," or a demagogue, according to the critic's political point of view. She conceded his integrity so far as money was concerned, and no doubt he was an able man, but his black frock coat vexed her soul. The skirts hitched in the back and sagged in front; never was it buttoned. His manners were like his coat, too individual to be pleasing. To women he paid no attention whatever, which to a woman is more offensive than rudeness itself. Once, he took Augusta out to dinner and talked all through the dinner to the man opposite. Augusta was not accustomed to have men take her out to dinner and talk to any one else. The sensation was new, but not agreeable. The single remark that he addressed to her was: "I see you ladies are bound to get your rights; you've another bill ready for the Legislature." To which Augusta had responded dryly: "Yes, I signed the petition against it." She did not notice the twinkle in his eye, because she was disdainfully eating her fish. Later, Win repeated to her the Senator's private counsel to the distracted legislators, who did not want to pass the bill nor to offend its promoters. "Well, boys," said he, "I can only recommend to you the advice of old Uncle Chet Tarbox, of Kansas, in the same case. 'That's easy,' says he, 'talk fur it and vote agin it!'"

"And he calls that principle?" Augusta sneered.

"No, dear, I think he calls it politics," said Win, "but he *is* a man of principles."

And now, just as the stakes were highest and he stood in to win, the poor fellow must drop out of the game. Augusta's heart softened to him. "And he knows it," she thought; "he has to lie there and dread the passage. At least Win was spared that. And that poor woman will have to help him. She doesn't strike me as a bit of a tower; poor, weak, conscientious thing! I suppose she is very religious; that kind of woman is likely to be. Well, I hope her religion will be a help to her," she sighed.

She drifted into a dreary reverie. The maid announced Miss Harmon twice before she heard. "It's Miss Harmon, ma'am. She said she knew it wasn't your day; but she'd be very much obliged if you would see her."

Augusta hesitated. She would have excused herself had she known any gracious way. Not knowing any, she bade the visitor be shown up. And she braced herself for the ordeal of sympathy.

The sunlight made a shining bar across the floor, which rose to the ceiling, in a wall of radiant mist filled with dancing, golden motes. She stood behind it, a slight and somber figure, with listless eyes. Through the mist the room was transfigured. The dull shine of the mahogany, the soft dazzle of the silver on her dressing-table, the roses of the wall-paper, the etching on the walls, the white curtains at the windows where the afternoon light had painted exquisite transparent shadows of violet; all these familiar things looked different and unreal. Unreal, also, looked the commonplace woman who advanced to her, her face illumined by that mystical glow. Augusta had a sudden impression of a new quality in it; it was as if, for the first time, she saw the real woman, not the exterior. And she remembered quickly their kinship in pain.

"I'm glad you came," she said, impulsively; "thank you for coming."

Miss Harmon stepped past the glow; she was her own, limp, neat, uninteresting self again. She seated herself in the manner taught her by the Delsarte teacher who had given the club lessons, and clasped her hands before her; and it was a second before Augusta realized that her silence came from the effort to master her emotion, and that the eyes behind her glasses were full of tears.

"I hope you will excuse me coming today," she began—evidently it was a little, carefully studied speech that she was reciting—"I appreciate how occupied you must be; I would not have intruded merely to express my—my deep sympathy. But my brother wished me to come. We were always interested in Mr. Winthrop Darcy. Brother was grateful to him, in the first place, that night he met me—the concert night when I was with a lady friend and we missed the street cars. I was very silly—

frightened; and he was so kind; he insisted on walking home with us, leaving his young friends. And I never was at any public entertainment that he didn't bow to me in the pleasantest manner. Brother appreciated it. And he appreciated your great kindness, too——"

"My dear, I never was kind," began Augusta. There had seemed to be a thin crust of ice over her sympathies, which used to run so quickly into any channel of need; but she thought to herself, "I always knew that shy woman was lonesome. Why didn't I be decent to her when I *could* feel!"

"And Brother always thought so much of you," continued Miss Harmon, innocently. For her the approbation of Roger Harmon was a crown to be coveted by the kings of earth. "Ever since one time that he took you out to dinner. He so liked your manners. And we used to like so much to watch Mr. Winthrop with you. We'd so often notice him at night before you pulled the shade down, his manner to you—I didn't mean to pain you. I can't tell you how sorry—I won't detain you, but it was so you would know why"—she had forgotten her studied phrases, her color flickered on her cheeks like a lamp-flame in the wind, she trembled—"so you would know why Brother wanted it. He thought it might comfort you; and whatever he asked me to do, I couldn't refuse."

"Surely not," said Augusta, gently, and she laid her hand on the trembling fingers lifted a moment, "but don't distress yourself, wait——"

"Oh, you are so good," sobbed Miss Harmon. "Oh, I can't wait, I have got to tell it quick for fear I'll break down. Don't be kind to me or I'll break down! I haven't broken down once. Nor cried. I don't dare to. This is what Brother asked me to tell you. 'She's a woman of sense,' said he, 'and she's on the blank side of the wall. She doesn't want to have folks talk to her when she knows they know as little as she does. I know how she feels. She can't talk. Why, it's not to be talked. It's unthinkable. You try to imagine where you'll be when you quit. You can't do it. You can't think yourself stopped—nothing!

BLANK SIDE OF THE WALL

You go to her, Sis,' he said, 'and you've a good memory, you give her exactly my words. She's a woman of sense; she won't talk any nonsense about maybe I'll get well. She knows I'm man enough to take my medicine without lies. Being a woman, what she wants most is to know that boy of hers is happy; being a woman, as much as she wants that, even more, maybe, she wants to do something for him. As long as you women can do something for those you love, you'll walk over red-hot coals and say it doesn't hurt. Well, I'll give her a chance to do something for him. I don't believe my soul is going to be done for entirely just because it has lost its job, here! I'm going on. You tell her I'll hunt her boy up. I'll find him. The will's going to count there as much as it counts here. You tell her I'll give him any message she wants to send. You tell her in just those words.' "

Miss Harmon had spoken in a voice as low and monotonous as a deaf man's. Her eyes were fixed and vacant. The color had concentrated in a single spot on her cheeks. One could see that she suffered frightfully, and did not know that she was in pain, so intent was she to obey. But at first Augusta hardly noticed her; the message was like a lightning bolt on a strange landscape in the night.

"He's right, he's right," she breathed, "if he only can!"

"Brother always does what he says he will," said Miss Harmon.

"And he is sure he will go on? Oh, how cruel I am to say that to you! You poor child!"

Impulsively she came to the other woman and put her arms about her. Miss Harmon's arms hung limply, but Augusta understood the strained whisper, "Don't be kind to me!"

"I won't. I know. And are you on the blank side of the wall, too? I thought that you were so religious."

"I used to hope I had faith, but everything is so dim now," Miss Harmon said, wearily. "My thoughts wander even when I try to pray. I'm no help to him, but"—a strange light dawned in her haggard face—"he doesn't need my help; he's finding it out

BLANK SIDE OF THE WALL

for himself. At first he said, 'It's tough. But we'll go through it, together, Sis. We've gone through everything together; we'll go through this.' But it has been he that helped me. He's thought of me all along. Doctor said that the first thing he said when he knew the truth was: 'Well, I always was glad I carried a big life insurance. Sis will be all right.' And only this morning, after I promised to come here, he said: 'Sis, when you come where I am you remember I said, "I mind it less every day."' I must be getting back, now. I can't bear to be away. When I'm with him, I'm quite calm, indeed I am, for I can see; but when I'm away I think of a thousand things. Will you tell him the message?"

Augusta drew a long breath. "Thank him, thank him from my heart. Tell him we will try to comfort each other. I can never forget his thought of me. And tell him to tell my boy that he blessed me all his life and that I know we shall be happy again."

Then, as Miss Harmon rose their eyes met. They went down the stairs together,

Augusta talking of other things—what neither of them ever knew. Augusta went up-stairs. When she returned, she stood for a moment before her boy's picture, looking steadily at the beautiful young face. "I believe I lied," she murmured, "just as I would have lied when you were dying if it would have helped you. 'The blank side of the wall?' Yes. He believed no more than I, and yet he is thinking it out, he thinks he will live."

Somehow the manner in which the dying man was planning his future as he would plan a journey, obscurely heartened her. It gave the homely comfort of a firelight shining from some cottage on a wanderer. The world where messages could be given and taken was not so aloof as it had seemed. "He can't know," she muttered; but she added, "He is on the very verge, surely he ought to see more clearly than we!" And, all at once, she found herself at the writing-desk writing to Miss Harmon. Afterward she was glad that she wrote those few words of gratitude, and asked if she might see the Senator. The reply came back immediately.

"My brother will be very glad if you will come to-morrow. He is feeling more comfortable, thank you. He told me to tell you to come in the morning, please."

Augusta was consumed with the miserable restlessness of grief all the evening. It was some diversion to drive to a florist. The windows were gorgeous with masses of lilies and golden jonquils. She remembered, when she saw them, that to-morrow was Easter. While she waited her turn at the counter she listened idly, yet with deepening interest, to a clerk explaining to a customer about the lilies. "You see," said he, "it's the same plant, just as much as a rose-tree is, if it does die down and there be nothing but a bulb left. It sprouts and the flower grows again."

Was there, she pondered, as her carriage rolled past the lights, was there any analogy between the lily and human life? Could there be, she wondered, some common meeting ground for all the souls that sought, no matter through what devious and varying paths, to find the eternal love? Was there a kinship among worshipers running deeper than any creed? How far was Win right and the sorrows that rend the heart, only the poignant but fleeting troubles of a child to be remembered with a smile?

She slept ill that night, but it would have been a new thing for her to sleep otherwise. At the same time, amid her distempered musings, she had the sensation of a lift to her thoughts. There was something different to think about instead of that old futile treadmill of misery.

The sunlight awoke her, and while she dressed she could hear the singing of birds. There was the brilliant languor of spring in the air, "the dear unrest," the clean splendor in the tints of earth and sky, the ineffable feeling of hope and resurrection that comes with every spring. She looked forward, actually she looked forward to her interview with Harmon. She leaned on the hope that was in her heart, and the beautiful morning was like an omen.

When she heard the chimes she perceived that she had slept later than usual. Their deep, keen resonance struck a silent chord in her heart. They were the chimes of her

BLANK SIDE OF THE WALL

own church, and they were playing a hymn that Win loved to hear her sing. It was not a distinctively Easter hymn, and she did not know that because of her and because of Win, whom he had loved, the rector had chosen it. Whether Win loved it for the music or the words she did not know, but she said the words over to herself with a thrill, wherein blended awe and remembrance and an unreasoning, timid hope.

> Thou hidden love of God whose height,
>   Whose depth unmeasured no man knows,
> I see from far thy beauteous light,
>   Inly I sigh for thy repose.
> My heart is pained, nor can it be
> At rest, till I find rest in thee!

As she said them she thought of Harmon. Had he, who seemed a hard man, even callous, had he perchance any moments when his soul leaned wistfully towards an unknown power that did not willingly afflict nor grieve the children of men, when it was comfort to him that he need not resent his fate? She was impatient to see him, to win from him any light that he might hold. All through her anguish she had neither prayed nor felt any inclination to pray. What came to her had assumed the air of the inevitable. She had so little confidence in any power of the spirit that she had had no thought to appeal to it. But while she walked over the elastic turf where the grass was springing, her eyes on the lilies that had died and bloomed again, she felt an impulse of her childhood before she tasted of the tree of knowledge.

"Oh, if it were any good to pray! If there were anybody!" she cried within. "I *want* to pray!"

By this time, being at the Harmons' gate, she raised her eyes, and the blood curdled in a flash about her heart, for on the door-knob hung a myrtle wreath, and the door stood open.

"I dared to hope; I was a fool," she said, with inexpressible bitterness. She was minded to turn and go back to the loneliness which was not to be lifted. But she remembered the dead man's sister. At least, in return for what they had meant to do, she would offer her ineffectual offices of kindness.

The old servant, with eyes swollen from weeping, met her at the door.

"I'm on the look-out for you, ma'am. I knew you'd come," she cried, "and poor Miss Lizzie, she left word she wanted to see you. Will you come up?"

"Wasn't it very sudden?" Augusta asked, feeling her nerves shrinking from the interview before her.

"Oh, very, ma'am; the heart failed, all of a minute, you might say. But oh, he didn't suffer; went off so peaceful. And she's been dreading him suffering at the end. And he had his senses. She was 'fraid at the end he'd be delirious. It's a great loss to the country, but no one knows what *we* lose but us."

She panted up the stairs while her grief thus found tongue. Augusta knew whose rooms they were passing and who lay behind that closed door. At the rustle of their passage, the door opened and Miss Harmon came into the hall.

Augusta had not thought how she should greet her, but at the sight of her face she took her into her arms without a word.

In a second, however, she saw that Miss Harmon was quite composed. "Will you come with me?" she said; she had no hesitation, no timidity now. "I have a message for you from him. You do not mind?"

"I came to see him," said Augusta; "I didn't know." She followed Miss Harmon into the room. Quietly she passed after her to her brother's side. Alive she had thought Roger Harmon ugly, almost coarse of aspect. The mask before her wore the mystical refinement of death. She noted it, but she noted more—the peace on the lined and rugged features of this elderly man of affairs was of the same quality and form as the peace on the beautiful young face of her son.

"Do they all smile like that when they are dead?" she thought.

Miss Harmon softly pushed a straying lock of the gray hair into place. She spoke—without emotion, her voice quite steady.

"I want to tell you about him. I told him what you said. He seemed so much better. It pleased him. 'You tell her I'll engage to do it,' he said. He was glad you

BLANK SIDE OF THE WALL

wanted to see him. 'She thinks I know something,' he said; 'sometimes I think I do myself. I know how little all this fret and sweat of ours is worth. And if this were the end of it, Lord, what a bungle the world would be! There must be something under it all. Now, there is nothing in this whole world that is destroyed; it only changes. Why should *we* be destroyed? Don't you worry, Sis; there is something a good deal bigger than the Presbyterian church, or any other church; and men have struggled to find it in all ages. And they do find it, when they die. Don't you worry, we'll talk this all over somewhere else. It's all right.'

"I longed so to talk with him, but I was afraid it might be bad for him; so I didn't. There was no reason to think he might not live weeks. But in the night the nurse called me. It came when he was asleep. He was unconscious. He—he never knew me after he kissed me good night that night. But—this is what I wanted to tell you—just before he died he opened his eyes, with such a bright, pleasant expression in them, as if he saw something, and he said: 'Well, *Winthrop!* Yes, I'll tell her.' That was all; he turned his head and sighed very softly and that was all."

Augusta did not move, did not speak; her only motion was to clasp more tightly the hand that trembled in her own.

Peace stole into her heart. Had this dying man seen her boy? It might be. She did not know; but an unearthly comfort born of something deeper than reason, tranquillized her pain; afar off she perceived the possibility of faith and hope. And it had come to her from this man whom she held so lightly! Yet in the repentance that swept over her there was no abasement; she felt that were he to know he would understand, and if a human soul would know and freely forgive should infinite comprehension be less kind? Unconsciously she sank on her knees, but the prayer on her lips was not in the majestic words that her childhood had learned. Hardly knowing that she prayed, there flowed from her soul the petition of the old Buddhist: "Forgive me, O Lord, as the friend forgives the friend, as the

BLANK SIDE OF THE WALL

father pardons his son, the lover his beloved!"

She arose, she bent reverently over the dead man, she kissed his hand. "My friend," she promised, "I will believe you. I am grateful."

Then she turned to Miss Harmon. "We are both alone," she said; "let us help each other."

At this moment the chimes began to ring; through the window she could see the eternal miracle of spring. The lilies burned in the sunlight, like white flame. A new meaning of Easter stole into her consciousness, even as light steals or the scents and sounds and mysterious stir of springtime, while the hymn sang itself in her heart.

> I see from far thy beauteous light,
>   Inly I sigh for thy repose.
> My heart is pained, nor can it be
> At rest till I find rest in thee.

PRINTED BY STROMBERG, ALLEN & CO
FOR
HERBERT S. STONE & COMPANY
PUBLISHERS
CHICAGO

www.ingramcontent.com/pod-product-compliance
Lightning Source LLC
Chambersburg PA
CBHW021822230426
43669CB00008B/834